The Strange World of David Lynch

The Strange World of David Lynch

Transcendental Irony from *Eraserhead* to *Mulholland Dr.*

ERIC G. WILSON

continuum

NEW YORK • LONDON

2007

The Continuum International Publishing Group Inc
80 Maiden Lane, New York, NY 10038

The Continuum International Publishing Group, Inc
The Tower Building, 11 York Road, London SE1 7NX

www.continuumbooks.com

Printed in the United States of America

Library of Congress Cataloging-in-Publication Data

Wilson, Eric G.
 The strange world of David Lynch : transcendental irony from Eraserhead to Mulholland Dr. / Eric G. Wilson.
  p. cm.
 Includes bibliographical references and index.
 ISBN-13: 978-0-8264-2823-3 (hardcover : alk. paper)
 ISBN-10: 0-8264-2823-1 (hardcover : alk. paper)
 ISBN-13: 978-0-8264-2824-0 (pbk. : alk. paper)
 ISBN-10: 0-8264-2824-X (pbk. : alk. paper)
 1. Lynch, David, 1946—Criticism and interpretation. 2. Motion pictures—Religious aspects. I. Title.

PN1998.3.L96W55 2007
791.4302'33092--dc22

                                                                    2007006464

Contents

Preface

The intense ambiguities of Lynch's greatest films have understandably generated a somewhat bewildering variety of interpretations. Some critics have focused on Lynch's connection to surrealist traditions. Other critics have interpreted Lynch's movies as parodies of other movies and cinematic genres. Still others have employed a poststructuralist model to illuminate the instabilities of Lynch. Yet others have used the psychoanalytical theories of Freud or Lacan to shed light on Lynch's connections between desire and fantasy. Some other critics have focused on Lynch's depictions of evil. Some have also meditated on Lynch's relationship to American culture. One critic has even detailed Lynch's conservative moral vision. Another—critic Martha Nochimson—has focused on Lynch's exuberant optimism: his faith in the redemptive romance of certain popular cultural images arising from the collective unconscious.[1]

I have drawn on many of these interpretive modes in my own reading of Lynch's films, especially the poststructuralist and psychoanalytical models and most importantly Nochimson's theory of Lynch's optimism. I argue that Lynch is a director committed to imagistic and linguistic instability. I also maintain that Lynch is interested in relationships between desire and fantasy. However, unlike most poststructuralist and psychoanalytical readers, I presuppose that these tendencies do not reveal Lynch's extreme skepticism toward meaning or his reduction of fantasy to wish fulfillment. On the contrary, I assume that for Lynch instability is liberating, a mode that transcends staid material conditions and possibly connects one to something like vital spirit. Likewise, I believe that Lynch's notions of fantasy push against constraining habits and potentially generate actual visions of being. These rather optimistic ideas relate this book firmly to the idea that Lynch is largely a romantic visionary, closer to Melville than to Breton, more in the line of Whitman than Lacan.

My argument, briefly, is this: Lynch, through his use of irony, unsettles cogent and often stifling ideologies and throws viewers into irreducible ambiguity, or a relentless interpretive limbo; however, this limbo is not a meaningless stasis but a rich abyss that approaches the no-thing that is being itself. In this way, Lynch's irony is transcendental. It pushes audiences into that borderland between equally valid though thoroughly opposed interpretations. Encouraging viewers into this realm, the films of Lynch invite ideas of a healing third term, a figure of synthesis that approximates traditional notions of self or soul. Hence, Lynch's pictures are, in this rather idiosyncratic fashion, religious: visions of how unsettling ambiguity can redeem one from oppressive conventions and free him into sublime realms, the precincts of the holy. In working to inspire such a state, Lynch's films are "Gnostic" in spirit—lessons in how to escape the willful laws of society's demiurges and in how to participate in seemingly infinite possibility.

These are admittedly bold claims concerning the power of the products of popular culture. I must confess that these assertions largely grow out of my own experiences of what in my mind are Lynch's greatest films: *Eraserhead*, *Blue Velvet*, *Wild at Heart*, *Lost Highway*, and *Mulholland Dr.* Watching these films, I feel as if I am ripped from my habitual ways of seeing the world and thrown into fresh potentials for being. I feel as though I've come face to face with some holy power, some ungodly god. I sense in this condition life's ultimate irony: no one representation, no matter how full and complex, can accurately capture the plenitude of being. I believe that everything on this earth—every creature and every word, each icon and each image—is a truth and a lie, a meaningful approximation of being and a meaningless veil covering life.

This book, then, grows more out of an existential experience than an academic theory. Indeed, the book might at times have an amateurish feel: it emerges from love more than from professionalism. In fact, I am a specialist neither in film studies nor in the study of religion. I am a specialist in literary Romanticism and a fervid lover of David Lynch. In putting these two conditions together—merging my profession with my passion—I have come up with this book, a book that will hopefully shed light on a key Lynchian current that has been largely overlooked or neglected: the current of transcendental irony, a religion that has nothing to do with religion.

In revealing this trend, I create a book that falls somewhere between an academic study and a trade book. The book in some ways is palpably academic. It offers original arguments concerning the meanings of Lynch's important films. It presupposes a basic understanding of Lynch's canon. And it engages other scholarship. However, at the same time, this study consistently nods toward a trade audience. It is cast in a jargon-free style. It spends some time summarizing complex parts of the films. It keeps most of the scholarly apparatus relegated to the endnotes.

Perhaps some might believe that this "tradish" aspect of the book leads me to make questionable scholarly connections. For instance, I relate Lynch's ideas of cinema to the Romantic irony of Friedrich Schlegel, a late eighteenth- and early nineteenth-century literary critic. I also place in dialogue Lynch's religious cinema and Rudolph Otto's early twentieth-century theory of the holy. Finally, I relate Lynch's cinematic rhetoric to Friedrich Schiller's late eighteenth-century notion of aesthetic play. One might quickly ask: why don't you read Lynch in the light of more historically appropriate contexts? Why do you not interpret his work as an example of Lacanian psychoanalysis or Deleuzian philosophy or the Reagan eighties?

The answer to these questions is rather simple: in forging connections that have little historical or cultural continuity, I'm actually following Lynch's lead. Recall that Lynch is a practitioner of the Transcendental Meditation of Maharishi Mahesh Yogi. As such, he is informed by an eclectic and perennial religious and philosophical tradition. Informed thus, he is very likely in his cinematic work to inflect ancient visions that by far pre-date his cultural and historical moment. In focusing on ideas analogous to these visions, I am trying to unearth intellectual contexts for Lynch's films that most have overlooked.

Indeed, in this book I attempt to cast Lynch as an original religious seer, an almost mystical presence who regardless of his immediate contexts creates artistic products that work to alter for the better our hearts and our minds. I believe that his obsessive strangeness produces a profound clarity, that his seemingly secular films promote something very close to soul. Admittedly, then, in analyzing Lynch I'm also advocating for him. I assume that his movies are ameliorative. I believe that his frames are raptures. If these presuppositions again place me in the camp of the amateur, I can only hope that my love is insightful, that my generalism is generative.

NOTES

1. John Alexander (*The Films of David Lynch* [London: Charles Letts, 1993]) is the leading exponent of the idea that Lynch is a surrealist. Kenneth C. Kaleta (*David Lynch* [New York: Twayne, 1993]) is especially sharp on how Lynch's pictures relate to other films and genres. Jennifer A. Hudson ("'No Hay Banda, and Yet We Hear A Band': David Lynch's Reversal of Coherence in *Mulholland Drive*," *Journal of Film and Video* 56, no. 11 [Spring 2004]: 17–24) is very good on Lynch's poststructuralist tendencies. Michael Atkinson (*Blue Velvet* [London: British Film Institute, 1997]) offers a beautiful meditation on Lynch and Freud, while Todd McGowan in "Lost on *Mulholland Drive*: Navigating David Lynch's Panegyric to Hollywood," *Cinema Journal* 43, no. 2 (2004): 67–89, and "Finding Ourselves on a 'Lost Highway': David Lynch's Lesson in Fantasy," *Cinema Journal* 39, no. 2 (2000): 51–73, provides insightful readings of Lynch and Lacan. Steven Jay Schneider ("The Essential Evil in/of *Eraserhead* [or, Lynch to the Contrary]," in *The Cinema of David Lynch: American Dreams, Nightmare Visions*, ed. Erica Sheen and Annette Davis, 5–18 [New York: Wallflower Press, 2004]) has an excellent essay on Lynch's vision of evil. Nicholas Rombes ("*Blue Velvet* Underground: David Lynch's Post-Punk Poetics," in *The Cinema of David Lynch: American Dreams, Nightmare Visions*, ed. Erica Sheen and Annette Davis, 61–76 [New York: Wallflower Press, 2004]) interprets Lynch's connections to seventies and eighties American culture. Jeff Johnson (*Pervert in the Pulpit: Morality in the Works of David Lynch* [West Jefferson, NC: MacFarland, 2004]) has discovered a reactionary moral vision in Lynch's films. Martha P. Nochimson in *The Passion of David Lynch: Wild at Heart in Hollywood* (Austin: University of Texas Press, 1997) has revealed the profoundly humanistic tendencies in the films of Lynch.

The Transcendental Irony
of David Lynch

Six Men Getting Sick

In 1966, during his second year at the Philadelphia Academy of Fine Arts, a young David Lynch decided to turn from painting to film. His first film, sometimes called *Six Figures* and other times termed *Six Men Getting Sick*, was made to be projected onto a special three-dimensional screen. This screen featured two extruding sculptures of agonized human faces. To the left side of these partial faces was a bust of a human head with its jaw pressed into its palm. At different times, the film projected three other faces to the right of these figures. Both the sculpted faces and the filmic faces came to life through animation. Bright red stomachs dropped down from the chins of the faces. Eventually, all the stomachs appeared to explode into flames. Then all six men seemed to vomit violently. The film ran for one minute. It was looped to play continuously. The only sound was a siren screaming in the distance.[1]

What can one say about this bizarre piece of filmmaking other than that it won a prize, launched Lynch's film career, and manifested his enduring interest in sounds and vomit? I suppose that one could say that the movie is a study of the interaction between stasis and motion: the stillness of the sculpted screen and the flux

1

of the moving images. One could further conclude that this film is a meditation on the interpenetration between the disgusting—projectile vomiting—and the beautiful—stomachs blooming to flame. One might moreover claim that this picture is a melding of the sacred and the profane—an apocalypse of purgative fire and a display of gross sensualism. Finally, one could opine that this is the typical Lynchian mixture of total silliness, the locker-room humor of puking, and complete seriousness, the Sartrean nausea of living absurdly.

Each of these responses would be valid but none would do justice to the utter strangeness of the images. Regardless of how hard one tries to interpret this film, one in the end remains disarmed, shocked anew with each turn of the loop. The hermeneutical antinomies ultimately cancel one another. Just when the viewer focuses on the meaning of one side—on motion or ugliness or horror or silliness—the other side overwhelms the scene: stillness crystallizes or beauty breaks through or the holy overwhelms or existential absurdity makes one sullen. The movie consumes itself, erases its own being. It becomes *no*-thing, a void beyond conception, emptiness: consuming nihilism. But the weirdness remains, the feeling that one has undergone an irreducibly unsettling *experience*. The experience, however, has been of no-*thing*, plenitude overwhelming categories, fullness: sublime being. *Six Figures* is both an annihilation of meaning and an overabundance of signification. It is the horror of hovering in the abyss and the exuberance of encountering spirit. It is against religion and profoundly religious. The viewer of the film cannot help but to be sick himself—sick of the excretions of the stupid world and sick of not experiencing this world with sufficient depth.

This opening moment in Lynch's filmography grants a brief glimpse into his overall nonsectarian religious vision—a vision of the holy based entirely on unmediated, unrepresentable, self-erasing *experience*. This religious vision is thus grounded on perception and form, attuned to how we apprehend the visible world and what forms our apprehensions take. This vision is therefore necessarily an ironic one, for all perceptions of forms are temporary, contingent, inaccurate—brief eddies in the great abyss of the cosmos, void and plenitude at once, nothing and everything.

The best thing to do now is to slow down and brood over this phenomenon that I am calling the ironic religion of David Lynch, a phenomenon that is complex to the core. Some preliminary remarks suggest this complexity. To say that ironic play generates religious experience is to suggest that religion can be grounded on the undoing of all forms. To claim that Lynch's films are religion, however ironic, is to assume that violent, sexual films are expressions of sublime holiness. To take this position on Lynch and religion is to presuppose two paradoxical theories that will be difficult to substantiate: a theory of "nonreligious" religious experience and a theory of a "sacred" secular cinema. Hopefully, this introduction will account for these complexities and clear a path for the first full-length study of the bizarre yet exhilarating religion of Lynch.

The Film before the Film

In the ironic religion of David Lynch, one great error is dualism, the division of the world into mutually exclusive opposites—good and evil, order and chaos. The other great mistake in Lynch's religion is monism, the reduction of the universe to unity without difference—spirit to matter or matter to spirit, form to turbulence or energy to structure. These two sins leave behind a seemingly impossible path to enlightenment, a way between or beyond one and many, harmony and discord. But what is there that does not participate in unity or diversity, order or chaos? The answer must be: nothing. Outside of dualism and monism is emptiness. The religion of Lynch is grounded on no ground. It is a blind vision. It is a hymn that no one can hear. It is the lost highway.

The religion of Lynch is dependent upon film. A film is a veil, a blockage between seer and seen. But a film is also a transparent medium through which one perceives light that would otherwise remain invisible. A film is moreover a motion picture, a series of static images on a celluloid strip whose quick turning gives the illusion of live action. But a film as cinematic roll is in addition a sequence of blank strips between pictures, voids required for the appearances of fullness. Film in Lynch's religion is thus opaque and translucent, hallucination and reality, form and emptiness.

Everything is a film—both dense to light and porous to illumination. A film is nothing—an absence at the core of being. This is the irony at the core of Lynch's religion. All film images are forms. All film images are empty. Form is emptiness; emptiness is form. The irony of this situation is a skeptical mode. It pronounces: events are appearances not connected to reality. But irony in this context is also a way of transcendence. It intones: no visible occurrence adequately represents the invisible absolute. This is the hopeless contradiction of this kind of ironic view: things are ephemeral illusions of an annihilating void; things are manifestations of an abyss of being. Everything is *no*-thing, meaningless. Each thing is no-*thing*, spirit.

The ironic religion of Lynch proposes that all religion is a theory of form. Orthodox religions—"exoteric" traditions—assume that one must follow specific forms to achieve salvation, sanctioned rites and rituals, appropriate worship and words. To follow such a religion, a "right-hand" path, is to bow to traditional representations of gods, to the structures of authority. Heterodox religions—"esoteric" currents—rebel against external forms and follow the inner energies, valuing spontaneity and whimsy. In practicing such a "religion"—really, "antireligion"—one presupposes that deity exists within the self, that authority is evil. In the context of form, this dichotomy between the right way of the moral religions and the left path of the immoral ones is false. Both conformist and rebel fetishize form, either worshipping or demonizing it.

The Lynch religion knows that fixation on form is death. Lynch's religion also realizes that rejection of form is impossible. This religion proposes a middle way between the exoteric, which sees form as ultimate, and the esoteric, which views form as insignificant. This middle path conceives of all forms as films: transparent and opaque, full and empty, real and illusory. Forms as films are as real as anything can be, patterns of experience, galvanizing facts. These forms are gorgeous or horrible circulations that run through the heart's core. But forms as films are also ghostly, phantom abstractions from the flux of existence, fictions. They delude insecure souls into believing in static ideas hovering above decay. One should embrace the form as an aesthetic event, a quick harmony of light and shade, silence and music. One should deny the form as a haunted concept, a hallucination of wispy smoke already fading into the void.

To care about form as real; to ignore form as illusion—this is, again, the basic irony of the religion of Lynch. This irony is best revealed through ironic filmic forms, strips of celluloid that annihilate themselves. Cinema rolls of the classical Hollywood type (the right-hand path of movies) attempt to reinforce conventional forms of life. These movies suggest that forms, including the images on the screen, are substantial. Celluloid strands of the avant-garde school (the cinematic left-hand path) try to destroy the collective structures of common sense. These films intimate that forms, even those composing the film itself, are phantom. The films of Lynch, the rites of his religion, feature the motifs of classical Hollywood and the disturbing breakages of the avant-garde. His films create forms so beautiful that they feel necessary and then destroy those forms as though they are nothing at all. His filmic forms reveal what is true of all forms as film.

The ironic religion of Lynch is aware of the original meaning of "religion," "to bind." Most obviously, religion as binding suggests that religion is constraint to a certain set of rules. Less obviously, binding in this sense intimates the double bind inspired by all forms, the desire to embrace forms as substances and the fear of forms as illusions. Even more subtly, the binding of religion hints at an unbreakable connection to a hidden origin that transcends all boundaries, all distinctions, and all forms.

To follow the religion of Lynch is to bind oneself to his filmic forms. This binding reveals the duplicity of all forms. Enduring this double bind might open one to a third term beyond the rift between many and one, chaos and order—a barely possible thing as lurid and gorgeous as blue velvet wavering in the muted light.

The Delicate Abstractions

These remarks on Lynch's religion are abstract. Not one of Lynch's feature-length films has been mentioned, nor have any of his views on Transcendental Meditation. It appears that this is an attempt to fit a secular filmmaker into a prefabricated theory of religion.[2]

However, these inaugural remarks on the ironic religion of Lynch partake of the spirit of Lynch's own thinking. In an interview, Lynch claims that his films cut against the grain of Hollywood conventions by focusing more on idea and image than plot and character. He says, "I love the delicate abstractions that cinema can do and only poets can do with words."[3] This exquisite phrase, "delicate abstractions," suggests an idea that is supple, lithe—a synthesis between mental vision and vibrant picture. That the refined idea is compared to the poem is significant. A strong poem is a series of disarming images expressing a complex idea. The idea is too paradoxical for simple narrative and thus requires dense images for its ambiguous expression. The image is too mysterious for simple allegory and therefore often gestures to rippling, barely graspable abstractions.

In another interview, Lynch describes his filmic images as mixtures of revelation and mystery. In composing these moving pictures, he is careful to keep from knowing too much about "what things mean or how they might be interpreted." If he did have a clear purpose in mind in making his films, he would be "afraid" to let the work be spontaneous, unexpected—to "let it keep happening." This "it" appears to be "mystery." A strict psychological reading of his images can destroy their "kind of magical quality." Once his forms are "reduced to certain neuroses or certain things," once these pictures are "named and defined," they lose their ambiguity and their "potential" for "vast, infinite experience."[4] Such an experience would be bounded and boundless at the same time, a finite event as well as an infinite rush. This is the potential of the "delicate abstraction," the picture that fades before the idea, the idea that dissolves into the image. This is the crepuscular mean between subconscious intention and conscious apprehension.

One interviewer describes a visit to an art museum with Lynch. There she and Lynch gaze at a Pollock painting. When the interviewer confesses that she doesn't understand the work, Lynch replies that she indeed does. He knows this because he can see her eyes "moving." As the interviewer concludes, this remark from Lynch presupposes a level of understanding below consciousness, a "subconscious" understanding.[5] Not "unconscious," this sort of apprehension *is* conscious but in a way that lies below mental representation. The eyes roving over a Pollock painting—both pattern and turbulence, too abstract for perception and too concrete for apprehension—spontaneously organize splotches of seemingly random color into somewhat cogent structures. These structures, however, escape stable representation. They engage the sight but elude the mind. But this engagement is meaningful—moving and magnetic. Currents of being below the radar of consciousness are energized. They direct the eyes to focus on this drift of color, that crossing of shade and light. The mind behind the eyes is baffled yet opened to depth and possibly heights that had heretofore been hidden.

In yet another interview, Lynch compares parts of his work to "B-film violence." He claims that he loves those "honest film-films which don't have any purpose other than being a film." The "film-film" is the standard for most all of Lynch's cinema.[6] Like Pollock, an artist of honest "painting-paintings," Lynch creates filmic forms that are simultaneously too concrete for easy abstract interpretation and too abstract for comfortable concrete perception. Such "delicate abstractions" appear, on the one hand, to be spontaneous, as random as the drifts of everyday experience. But, on the other hand, these same images seem to express order, some invisible end just beyond the eye's gaze and the mind's reaching. As Lynch confesses in still another interview, his mode of composing a feature-length film is to get ideas for seventy scenes and to put these ideas on index cards.[7] This method suggests that Lynch's films grow from a negotiation between unexpected images arising from the subconscious and disciplined organizations of the conscious mind. This is a tense negotiation. The unpredictable particulars upset the whole and the holistic principle subdues the particulars.

Between Formalism and Realism

What do Lynch's tensions between parts and wholes have to do with religion? To answer this question, one must pause on the enduring split in film criticism between formalism and realism.[8] The earliest defenses of the artistic value of film were based on comparisons between cinema and the visual arts. The first apologists for film as art watched their favored medium emerge at the same time as schools of nonobjective painting—including surrealism, Dadaism, and cubism. Basing their ideas on these forms of art, these apologists praised the transformative power of the moving image, the fact that the filmmaker could shape his cinematic world to fit his abstract idea. Early theorists like Rudolf Arnheim, Ernest Lindgren, Sergei Eisenstein, and Vsevelod Pudovkin came to the same conclusion: if film is to be accepted as art, it must avoid objective representation and instead endeavor to transmute image into idea. The cuts of montage are superior to the unfolding of recorded time. Georges Méliès' supernatural *Trip to the Moon* trumps the Lumière Brothers' empirical *Arrival of a Train.*[9]

In the middle of the twentieth century, certain critics countered the formal theory of cinema. Constituted by André Bazin, Henri Agel, Alain Bandelier, and Siegfried Kracauer, this realist school distinguished film from painting by espousing the keen objectivity of mechanical recording. The film records the world through chemical processes; thus, it removes the observer and therefore offers a medium grounded on the absence of the subject. Film grants the artist the possibility of disclosing the world, not simply interpreting it. The film does not represent reality. It presents the real.[10] The emphasis on the correspondence between film and reality favors mimetic films and documentary style films. It chooses the classical Capra over the avant-garde of Welles.

The ideas of Bazin and his followers inspired a theory of film *as* religion. Amédée Ayfre argued that films can only be significantly religious through a realistic style. Truly religious films— which need not depict obvious religious themes at all—record the world directly. They aspire for this immediate presentation in order to reveal the mystery of the real. This notion is grounded on paradox: the filmmaker transcends the image through the image. Focusing his work on naked materiality, the director calls attention to the density of things. This transformation of typical objects into striking occurrences inspires wonder. As one critic has claimed, Ayfre's theory of "spiritual realism" requires that the holy be understood through both "the incarnational (a rootedness in reality itself) and the transcendent element (a self-negating quality discernible in reality)." Films instancing this "spiritual

realism" are Bresson's *The Diary of a Country Priest* and Dreyer's *The Passion of Joan of Arc.*[11]
This theory of spiritual materiality highlights only one side of the issue. What of the sacred possibilities of surrealism, of montage, of camp?[12] The realist religious film reveals the sacred through opacity, the mystery of the dense. In contrast, the nonobjective religious picture discloses the ineffable by way of transparency, the mystery of illusion. Films pushing against realism are skeptical toward the idea that the empirical world is substantial. The surrealist picture believes that reveries brimming up from the unconscious are more authentic than the facts of consciousness. Filmic montage suggests the primacy of the mind over events. The campy film claims that behaviors are clichéd performances and not authentic actions. Each of these modes emphasizes the mental over the physical. Films in these styles can be cynical toward transcendence; they assume that we are trapped in the delusions of our own minds. However, these movies can also be transcendental, for they presuppose the insubstantiality of the visible and inspire viewers to explore the invisible—the unconscious, the mind. A film instancing this "spiritual formalism" renders the event transparent to impalpable energies. This drainage of solidity disorients audiences and throws them into nothing in particular—the undifferentiated plane that might be spirit itself. Examples of this "spiritual formalism" are Antonioni's *Blow Up* and Fellini's *8½.*

Spiritual realism emphasizes matter over mind. Spiritual formalism does the opposite, valuing mental action over material stasis. The realistic cinema of the sacred is committed to incarnation, a Catholic notion of transcendence of world through embrace of the world. Formalistic sacred cinema is devoted to antimatter, a Gnostic idea of transcendence of world through rejection of the world. If the realist stares at one object until it becomes luminous, then the formalist only glances before leaving the thing behind as nothing. Where the realist thirsts for the simple, the formalist revels in the complex.

The reason I have described these realist and formalist tendencies—admittedly in a somewhat reductive way—is that I want show how Lynch's particular style places realism and formalism into a tense, conflicted relationship and how this relationship produces what I have been calling the ironic religion of Lynch. The primary feature of Lynch's interplay between spiritual realism and spiritual formalism is irony. This irony is of a particular kind. This is the special sort of irony developed by Romantic theorists at the turn of the nineteenth century: irony as a path to transcendence.

Transcendental Irony

Irony exists in the gap between appearance and reality. Certain thinkers at the end of the eighteenth century, namely Friedrich Schlegel, thought that this gap is the primary feature of the human condition, an antagonism between the desire to represent the world and the inability to do so. The only way to transcend this conflict, Schlegel believes, is to become aware of it, to undercut representations the instant they are posited. This perpetual creation and destruction leads to vital participation in the energies of the cosmos, itself a constant metamorphosis from form to formless, formless to form.

The exemplar of this kind of irony is the Socrates of Plato's dialogues. Socratic irony is the "only involuntary and yet completely deliberate dissimulation." Both "perfectly instinctive and perfectly conscious philosophy," Socrates' method grows from his raw desire always to know more and his studied performance of ignorance. The authentic passion for knowledge overwhelms the unstudied persona while the mask of ignorance covers the deep knowing. This opposition between the quest for truth and the feigning of stupidity "arouses a feeling of the indissoluble antagonism between the absolute and the relative, between the impossibility and the necessity of complete communication." This is the tension of all gestures, all utterances: between the fullness of the cosmos's becoming and the fragments by which humans attempt to represent this abundance. To become conscious of this conflict and to enact it oneself through "continuous self-parody" is to achieve freedom from fixation on any one representation and to suffer the limitation of never knowing anything finally.[13]

Though skeptical of reaching the absolute, this irony is "transcendental."[14] In measuring the real against the ideal and the ideal against the real, this irony never becomes fixed on one form. Irony of this sort turns into a sort of sacred buffoonery, a boundless jest never seriously moored in the world. Destroying as it creates, standing in itself and outside of itself, this kind of irony approaches the infinitude of self-consciousness, the mind's ability to think and watch itself think. This is the terror of never being able to rest on any representation of the world, the joy of escaping any final structure.

One persistent motif in Schlegel's kind of irony, especially in its Socratic form, is this: one is never entirely sure if it's present or not. This distinguishes romantic irony—philosophical, poetic, and religious seeking—from what I'll call instrumental irony—a stylistic method good for rather obvious satire. To understand this distinction, let's take some cinematic examples of the latter sort of irony.

Let's take Woody Allen's *Annie Hall*.[15] This film is filled with ironic devices. The protagonist, played by Allen, turns to the camera and comments on his character. Characters enter into flashbacks and interview characters from the past. An animated sequence provides interpretation of the live action narrative. A final scene features the rehearsal of a play retelling the movie's story but with a happy ending. Each of these elements highlights the fact that this film is an artifice, one of many possible images of "reality." This emphasis on the tenuous nature of this imitation works for comic purposes—humorously to deflate cinematic conventions that support stable identity and linear narrative. The irony is obvious and uncomplicated, designed mainly to get laughs.

Instrumental irony is not always comic. Let's turn to Quentin Tarantino's *Kill Bill*. Every scene appears to be a pastiche of a moment from seventies popular culture: kung fu movies, spaghetti westerns, blaxploitation films, and neo noir. These quotations of other films undercut the authenticity of the movie. They emphasize the possibility that every event is a simulacrum of pop cultural images, themselves simulacra of yet other elements of pop culture. This is the Baudrillardian world of the postmodern, a flattening of depths to surfaces. As in the case of Allen's film, the irony is obvious, this time not for laughs but to revel in the campy culture of the seventies.

Instrumental irony can escape comedy and glibness. It can bear serious meanings. Recall the films earlier mentioned as examples of "spiritual formalism," experimental pictures that undercut cinematic expectations in an effort to question the status quo. We think of 8½, a surrealistic dream that forces us to question the waking world and possibly to seek for deeper reality. We also notice *Blow Up*, which blurs the distinction between art and life and makes us wonder if reality is illusion and illusion real. These subtle films—parodying reality with dream and dream with reality—find worthy imitations in the work of Tom Tykwer, whose *Run Lola Run* blurs reality and reverie.

These profound films are close to romantic irony. Blurring the "natural" and the "artificial," they upset habitual relationships to the world and force new ways of seeing. Still, these pictures remain outside of the thoroughly ambiguous atmosphere of romantic irony through their rather obvious uses of irony as one instrument among many. In contrast, the film fraught with romantic irony is never obviously ironic. Filmmakers who share with Lynch a mastery of this mode are Stanley Kubrick and Jim Jarmusch. Watching Kubrick's *Eyes Wide Shut*, we are never sure if we should take seriously Tom Cruise's character, Dr. Bill Harford. Does Kubrick mean for us to take Cruise's wooden acting as an earnest depiction of a sexually repressed, death-loving physician, or does he want us to view this seemingly bad acting as a parody of typical American maleness? Or, more troublingly, does Kubrick intend for us to take the character both ways at once? We experience similar confusions viewing Jarmusch's *Dead Man*. We wonder throughout if this picture is a pure parody of the Hollywood western or a subtle spiritual meditation on the West as an unbounded realm. Can the film be parody and parable at the same time? Can it erase itself, kill itself, and leave nothing in its wake but a dead man?

Certain Lynch pictures are similar. They leave us wondering if we've experienced an awesome meditation on being or a silly avoidance of the serious. We can never be sure if we're meant to cower before the sublime or laugh our heads off. This bizarre irony necessarily brings to mind holy images, sites that both posit their powerful existence but also dissolve before the divine as ridiculous fogs. Standing before such a holy pattern, we want to quake with both fear and laughter. We are afraid of our insignificance before this immensely potent image. We get tickled over the pomposity of this same image, for it looks funny when compared to the divine power it wishes to represent. Such is the holiness of transcendent irony, a mode that dwells in the middle of the overflowing, beautiful light and the tawdry lightbulb trying to capture the current.

Ironic Religion

Religious irony is nonsectarian. It is not tied to one tradition or another but eclectically spans the spectrum of religious expression. It appears wherever the religious seeker attempts the paradoxical middle path between engagement and indifference. Aware of this seemingly irreducible gap between representation and the unrepresentable, this seeker defines the holy as an event in which the gap is revealed, in which what is always already true of everything else is brought into blinding light. This seeker hungers for sites that essentially erase themselves, that posit their being just as they are undone by the abyss on which they float. Experiencing these sites—which can be traditional religious images but also aesthetic objects such as poems or paintings or films—the seeker apprehends his own relationship to the boundless energies of the cosmos. He senses that he himself is but a temporary pattern of a massive energy, an eddy in an immense ocean. He partially expresses the depths but at the same time blocks their mysteries. He yearns for a third position that might bring these two poles together.

Ironically—in the sense that it's the opposite of what's expected—the theory of religion that comes closest to this nonsectarian ironic perception is Rudolph Otto's idea of the holy, developed during the first quarter of the twentieth century. On the surface, Otto's ideas on the numinous are very far from irony. Otto argues that the essence of religious experience in any tradition is a seizure of sorts, a moment when a creature is "submerged and overwhelmed by its own nothingness in contrast to that which is supreme above all creatures."[16] Such an experience of profound awe—one in which the beholder is fully engaged— appears to have very little to do with transcendental irony, a mode that is as detached as attached. However, a closer look will reveal this: Otto's theory of the numinous is in fact a deep example of romantic irony. His theory dwells in the gap between the desire to represent and the failure of representation, full attraction and total rejection, participation and separation. Dwelling in this gap, this theory illuminates Schlegel's transcendent irony as well as Lynch's ironic films. Otto's ideas in the end reveal the effects of especially ironic events—events such as powerfully ironic films, events like Lynch's pictures.

According to Otto, certain images, regardless of space and time, have been simultaneously embraced and feared as sites of the "numinous." This term details an experience of the holy. This experience occurs when a person feels insignificant in the face of a superabundant power that transcends the visible cosmos. This feeling is a subjective and an objective event. The person feels the *numen*—the overwhelming and holy power, the *mysterium tremendum*—to be both outside the self and inside the self, both a transcendent plenitude and a ubiquitous current. Characterized by "awe," "majesty," and "energy," the numinous experience is not rational, not predictable.[17] It is an ungraspable and shattering encounter with a "wholly other" that is somehow deeply, mysteriously the same. This duplicity is a mixture of pleasure and pain. The beholder of the numinous is pleased over being energized by a vital power, but he is pained over his inability to represent this power. He must accept the ironic predicament of the human condition. No one image, however rich, can accurately reveal ultimate being.

Otto illuminates this gap between desire and fulfillment when he compares the numinous to Kant's late eighteenth-century sublime.[18] Both the numinous and the sublime point to awesome, "mind-blowing" experiences in which one undergoes pain and pleasure—pain at being overtaxed by unrepresentable energies, pleasure at intuiting the transcendent.[19] The numinous and the sublime are not "physical" or "phenomenal" experiences. They are encounters of principles—such as the "absolute" or the "abyss"— that cannot be represented by empirical or imaginal faculties.

These principles can only be intuited by the reason. Yet, though
the sublime (and, analogously, the numinous) occurs internally
and cannot be attached to one image or another, certain images
are more likely to inspire the sublime feeling than others. Kant
suggests that the nebulae, the ocean, the vast cathedral each features physical qualities that make it a likely *site* of such staggering
experiences.[20]

Like Kant's cathedrals and nebulae, Lynch's religious films are
numinous. They unsettle viewers with their overabundant significations, their endless interplays between opposing meanings,
between surface and depth, content and form. Beholding this cinematic dynamism, one is made to feel that no one representation
can ever accurately portray the imagistic potency, the formal turbulence. Yet while one is pained over his inability to make sense of
what he witnesses, one at the same time feels pleasure over a new
sensibility: a feeling that he too participates in this crushing
power, that he is a pattern of its force. Attracted and repelled, one
is pulled asunder between known and unknown, image and abyss.
He yearns for some miraculous concept that might bring these
antinomies into some sort of harmony, a concord that retains the
power of both without losing the virtues of either. He pines to
play in the middle ground.

Aesthetic Play

I have claimed that these various polarities—between the unconscious and consciousness, appearance and reality, pattern and
abyss—inspire viewers to reach after a third term that might make
them feel, for a time, whole. What is the nature of this third term?
It is difficult to say, for this third position is almost always an
ideal, an ungraspable state of perfection frequently likened to the
complete self or the vital soul. However, I can claim this: the third
term, whatever shape it takes, must be serious and playful at once,
simultaneously attached and detached, ironic to the core.

Around the same time that Schlegel was developing his theories of irony, Friedrich Schiller was thinking about his own theory of aesthetic play. His idea of play articulates the structure of
all dynamic mediation. In Schiller's view, play, or the aesthetic

sensibility, discovers a way to bring oppositions into a vital harmony in which one appreciates the virtues of both poles without
suffering the limitations of either. To achieve this balance, one
must embrace and reject both poles, must take an ironic stance
toward each. Achieving this position, one through aesthetic perception or activity enjoys, however briefly, the elusive third term.
Lynch's films, I believe, inspire viewers to reach for this playful
position. In doing so, these pictures offer audience members an
approximation of what it must be like to experience the desideratum of most religions: self or soul—wholeness, synthesis, even
mercy and redemption.

For Schiller, most people are obsessed with sensuality or
rationality. The person overcome by the sense drive is concerned
only with "physical existence" or "sensuous nature." This person is
set "within the bounds of time" and therefore little different from
matter. He is determined, pulled into the flows of ephemeral
material. Participating in processes beyond his control, he is,
despite his attachment to organic currents, little different from
the machine. In contrast, if one is bent on the form drive, he associates with a rational principle above vicissitude. He believes that
his reasonable ego is an eternal substance untouched by accidents
of matter. He thinks he is free, beyond nature. Straining to control
his environment, he dreams of humanism, the sovereignty of
man. Both the formal theorist and the sensual practitioner are
limited, attaching themselves to one half of existence and ignoring
the other. The sensuous person is confined to matter at its lowest
level. He is but a cipher for his environment. The formal subject is
moored to his concepts. He is trapped in his mind.[21]

For Schiller, one escapes these binds through the play drive:
the energy behind the contemplation, embodiment, or creation of
beauty. Engaging in aesthetic activities, one finds "a happy mid-
way point between law and exigency"—between the abstract and
the concrete, structure and content. The playing person draws
from the powers of the sensual and the formal, but he is bound to
neither. He realizes that the sensual, when measured against ideas,
becomes "*small*," and that reason, when related to perceptions,
grows "*light*." He places the formal and the sensual into a creative
dialogue in which one side delimits and ennobles the other. He

knows that each impulse is required for beauty, but that neither alone can provide aesthetic education.[22] This aesthetic vision, this third term within yet beyond content and form, requires an irony: the ability to take the antinomies of existence at once seriously and in jest. Think of it: you are watching a Lynch film. You are immediately pulled in by his gorgeously weird colors and obsessively unsettling noises. You could spend hours simply enjoying his images and intonations. But then you realize that this light and sound show coheres into certain repeated forms, certain static rhythms—conceptual meanings. You pull away from the immediate contact and begin to search for rational significations. You realize the joy of interpretation and the limitations of raw experience. After a while, though, you feel that forms without content are vapid, that meanings without turbulence are static. You yearn again for the colors and noises, but this time you don't go after them with total intensity. You hold back, ever so slightly, not taking these lights and sounds as seriously as you did before. You find that you soon pine once more for the joys of interpretation, and so you return. This time, however, you don't want to leave behind the lubricious content. You embrace the meaningful forms, but not as tightly as before; you don't take these stable rhythms quite so seriously. Simultaneously accepting and rejecting both poles, you discover a dynamic middle ground between the two, a site where the virtues of content energize form, where the powers of form vitalize content. Attached yet unattached, you can play with each pole without becoming consumed by either. You are free from the terrible opposition that earlier plagued you. You feel for a time harmonious, settled, perhaps even happy.

According to Schiller, all great works of art achieve this melding of sensual and formal and thus inspire in their beholders this playful interaction. However, some works of art are simply more playful than others and thus more likely to foster an awareness of the dynamics of play. Romantically ironic works of art—like those of Lynch—would certainly constitute striking examples of these more playful works. Beholding works of romantic irony places sensitive interpreters in strange positions. On the one hand, the interpreter of an ironic work of this kind is seduced by the most apparent level of meaning, the sweet surfaces that seem immediately to make perfect sense. On the other hand, this same interpreter is repulsed by this surface and pushed to ungraspable depths, to unrepresentable powers that perpetually undercut the simple sheens. Pulled asunder, he is encouraged to discover the ideal third term. He self-consciously seeks this term, and likely finds it in the playful interaction between surface and depth, obvious and latent, pattern and abyss. He realizes that the surface requires for its seductions the depths and that the depths need for their potencies the surface. One side negates the other; one side needs the other. Realizing this ironic tension, the witness of the work might for a brief period come to enjoy the virtues of surface and depth without becoming constrained to either. He might participate in the dynamic middle ground between the two extremes, the borderland where one can be two things at once and neither thing at all.

Romantically ironic works of art—like certain films of Lynch—constitute special invitations to play. They encourage their audiences to seek those blissful moments in which for a brief second all wounds are healed. Fostering this harmony, works inducing ironic play function as do traditional notions of soul or self. Over the centuries, especially in Gnostic, Neoplatonic, and alchemical circles, the soul has been viewed as a mediating power, a potency capable of bringing into dynamic concord matter and spirit, time and eternity. Studied in the soul, certain more secular thinkers such as Carl Jung have claimed that the self is this mediating term, an entity that brings into tense synthesis consciousness and the unconscious, ego and abyss. Regardless of what one calls this mediating power—self, soul, or play—it creates for a moment what we might call mercy, a respite from the burdens of time, or redemption, an elevation above the rips of history.

Transcendental Meditation

In a 2005 interview, Lynch beautifully consolidates irony, the holy, and play in the relationship between his religion and his filmmaking by discussing his spiritual commitment. Since the early 1970s, when he was making *Eraserhead*, Lynch has been a devotee of Maharishi Mahesh Yogi and his method of Transcendental Meditation. Based on the Hindu discipline of yoga, this form of meditation is simple. For twenty minutes a day, the practitioner sits with his eyes closed and repeats his one-syllable mantra. This mantra is designed to focus the mind on one idea and thus to inspire a feeling of unity. This feeling is supposed to breed relaxed, passive acceptance of the way things are, openness to the flow of thoughts and things gently balanced between attachment and detachment. Allegedly, this condition allows the body to gain a deeper state of relaxation than it gets in regular sleep. But this state also apparently increases mental awareness and focus, empowering the practitioner to experience the world more vividly.[23]

Lynch maintains that this nonsectarian religious practice has opened him to an idea of God as a "totality" beyond any one name. He calls this divinity the "almighty merciful father, and the divine mother, the kingdom of heaven, the absolute, divine being, bliss consciousness, creative intelligence." This God is "unchanging, eternal." It "is," yet it is also "nothing." Awareness of this full void has expanded Lynch's consciousness. He believes that "there's just too much happiness and consciousness and wakefulness and understanding growing" for anyone to be "suffering so much, or caught up in some narrow little thing." Part of this expansion is his appreciation for many kinds of religious seeking. He suggests all religions at root are devoted to "mystery" and to turning their practitioners into "seeker[s]." This feeling of expansion, this understanding of religions, Lynch further claims, often just "happens," unexpectedly and spontaneously. One suddenly wants "to know," to "experience," to "learn about things."[24]

Lynch describes the feeling he has at times achieved while meditating. Sometimes, when the "experience" "kicks in," he undergoes "intense bliss," as if "the unbounded ocean" had poured into him. This condition is called "bubbling bliss," a sensation that has made Lynch feel as though he is a lightbulb flooded with light and capable of passing this light out into the world. This theory of intensifying the ubiquitous light is connected to the global environmentalism of Transcendental Meditation, the idea that meditation ameliorates the natural and political state of the world.[25]

Most importantly, Lynch's meditation has played a major role in his creativity. While meditating, he sometimes sinks into a "field of pure creativity," the "source" from which ideas come. His egocentric "anxieties and fears" fade away, and he dissolves into a subconscious realm that resembles a "pure open channel of ideas." Out of these experiences grow what Lynch most loves—those delicate abstractions. Though films should not be solely made of abstractions, pictures that "hold" abstractions delight him. These abstract pictures, he suggests, evade clear meanings and instead inspire rich feelings. These delicate abstractions—feelings more than thoughts—are, Lynch claims, like "seeds," or, more interestingly, like the "Vedas, the laws of nature."[26]

These are remarkable claims, even if they are articulated in a casual newspaper interview. They intimate, on the one hand, that the imagistic ideas that arise during meditation are manifestations of stable, unchanging laws. On the other hand, these statements suggest that the delicate abstractions of meditation are inflections of wispy, lubricious feelings. The picture of the meditator as a bulb overflowing with light captures this duality: the adept is a pattern of the whole, a revelation of pervasive consciousness, but also a condensation of the boundless, a distortion of the absolute. Lynch's remarks on meditation—appropriately serious and casual at the same time—partake of the spirit of Schlegel's theory of irony, Otto's idea of the holy, and Schiller's notion of play. Lynch's thoughts suggest that the religious seeker should take his relationship to spirit very seriously, for he is a unique manifestation of this numinous power. However, Lynch's ideas also intimate the opposite. Because the seeker is ultimately an incomplete and inaccurate representation of the numinous, he should not take his connection to spirit very seriously at all. In fact, he should reject his relationship as much as embrace it. Finding himself in this strange middle ground between extremes, he must reach for the healing third term that might redeem him from his chronic wound. This term might be, as I've intimated, something akin to a synthesizing self or to some notion of soul.

The conclusion to Lynch's interview nicely encapsulates this earnest playfulness. When asked if his films reflect the principles of Transcendental Meditation, Lynch responds in the negative, claiming that movies that exemplify a "message" are as uninteresting as telegrams. He then emphasizes that his films actually have nothing to do with his "religion." "Film," he observes, is not a vehicle to "sell" his religious "thing," but an expression of "ideas" that he has "fallen in love with." If Transcendental Meditation does appear at all in his films, it shows through in an inadvertent, "innocent" way.[27] Obviously, on the one hand, Lynch's movies are not mere narrations of the religious dogmas of Maharishi Mahesh. However, on the other hand, his films are sites of Transcendental Meditation—representations of the ideas arising from Lynch's meditations as well as realizations of the ironic interplay between emptiness and form. The appearance of his "religion" in his films is indeed "innocent": it is an accidental upsurge of the subconscious (Lynch doesn't intend to make movies on religion); it is an organic expression of his inner life (Lynch can't help but make religious films).

Five Ironic Images

I've taken a brief newspaper interview too seriously. I've treated casual journalism as a rich instance of the religious "thought" of David Lynch. I've even compared this interview to Schlegel's irony, Otto's holy, and Schiller's play. We should discount most of what I've written and now turn again to a discussion of some films.

But perhaps we should take my remarks in earnest, for it is certainly possible that Lynch's off-handed utterances during this interview are profound, if indirect, revelations of his theory and practice of filmmaking. The problem is, we can never know. Recall Schlegel's take on the ironic practices of Socrates: no one knows when to take the philosopher seriously and when to assume he's joking.

We probably do have this difficulty when we watch a Lynch film. We wonder, is he joking or what? Whether this ambiguity grows from Lynch's meditating or not is finally not that important. What is important, and interesting, is the "religious" density of Lynch's ironic style—how it, regardless of its origin, works to place audiences in a fecund limbo between seemingly irreconcilable opposites and possibly to seek a redemptive third term, a sacred no-thing beyond and within all strife.

Certain films in Lynch's canon prove especially mesmerizing exemplifications of this uncanny sort of irony. A quick glance at some of Lynch's weirdly shimmering endings gives a glimpse into these rich tensions between form and formless, pattern and void. What follows is a gallery of moving images, rendered (ironically) in words.

Eraserhead (1977) concludes with the forlorn Henry seemingly crashing through the dark shell in which he has been imprisoned and merging with the weirdly angelic chanteuse dwelling in his old radiator. Is this final scene a sign of Henry's madness, his giving over to his nocturnal illusions, or is it a moment of legitimate transcendence, a man discovering pure light in the grimiest corner?

The last image in *Blue Velvet* (1986) depicts Dorothy playing in a park with her son, recently restored to her after having been kidnapped. Though she appears to be happy, her melancholy eyes are portentous, as is the heartbreaking version of "Blue Velvet" that croons as the camera moves slowly toward the sky. This could be another of the film's many scenes of repression—Dorothy, a mentally ill sexual masochist, can never really find happiness—but it could also be an instant of purity emerging from pollution—Dorothy recovers an identity as holy mother, the blessed virgin untouched by biology.

The conclusion of *Wild at Heart* (1990) features Sailor returning to his beloved Lula. He had abandoned her only minutes before but comes back after having a vision of the Good Witch of the North. He finds Lula and his son stranded in traffic, lifts Lula onto the hood of the car, and sings to her "Love Me Tender." Is this meant to be a parody of the happy endings of Elvis films, or is it intended as a culmination of the spiritual journey, an attainment of enlightenment at the end of the yellow brick road?

Lost Highway (1997) ends with Fred driving at night down a lonely highway. He has already allegedly killed his wife, transformed into another man, repeated some of the ills of his former identity, and turned once more into his old self. As he stares blankly into the cold darkness, we wonder if he has been condemned to hell on earth, to an endless journey over a wasted desert. But we also imagine that he might have broken out of the vicious cycle of repeated mistakes to a plane where time has no meaning.

The conclusion of *Mulholland Dr.* (2001) is one of Lynch's most cryptic. The characters of the labyrinthine plotlines have all faded away, and we find ourselves in an old theater, the Club Silencio. A woman with blue hair and a white face appears in the balcony. She whispers, "Silencio." The film ends. This image emphasizes the artificial quality of the movie, the fact that it is a construct occurring in a theater. But this startling picture also suggests that this silent theater is reality itself, the third realm generating and destroying both illusion and fact, mere mimicry and moving experience.

These moments and these comments provide only slight indications of the ironic richness of Lynch's religious films. To feel the curious depths and glaring heights of Lynch's religious vision, one would have to live with each of these films for a long time and write about them over several pages. During this study, one would find that each of these pictures explores the complexities of a different religious motif, an archetypal spiritual situation. *Eraserhead* meditates on the primal decline and return of the Gnostic cosmology: the fall into dark matter and the possibility of redemption through denying this same sable material. *Blue Velvet* inflects the motif of the blessed virgin, based on the idea that the spiritually troubled male can find salvation only by way of a spiritually pure female presence. *Wild at Heart* is a Lynchian retelling of the redemptive power of romantic love—a meditation on the idea that the open heart is the way to God. *Lost Highway* renders the most harrowing of religious notions: negative theology, the theory that one can only know God through what God is not, that extreme confusion and loneliness are the only paths to knowledge and communion. *Mulholland Dr.* details the dream vision, grounded on the idea that the images arising from sleep elevate the soul to heavenly, potentially redemptive sights unavailable to the waking consciousness.

Each of these films is, in a certain way—like *Eraserhead*—Gnostic. Each inflects, however indirectly, a certain motif from the Gnostic tradition. *Eraserhead*'s Gnosticism is obvious. *Blue Velvet*'s is less so, but still draws on the Gnostic idea of the eternal feminine. In the same indirect way, *Wild at Heart* depicts a Gnostic situation: wild, sensual love might be a path to spiritual transcendence. *Lost Highway* likewise uses a Gnostic theme: one can know reality through negation, through canceling concepts inadequate to reality's superabundance. Finally *Mulholland Dr.* reflects the Gnostic idea that all reality is really a dream.

That each of these films in some way inflects a Gnostic motif is appropriate, for Gnosticism is a prime example of nonsectarian religious irony. Eschewing cogent religious faiths like Judaism or Christianity, Gnosticism focuses on raw experience with the divine, on intimate acquaintance that breeds knowledge, *gnosis*. However, the Gnostic tradition knows that this acquaintance can never be full. The object of the experience—the absolute—is always beyond full comprehension. This *gnosis* is thus ironic: both knowledge and ignorance, light and darkness.[28]

I'm of course not in any way trying to suggest that Lynch was or is a student of Gnosticism. What I am attempting to argue is this: those Gnostic situations that I detailed above prove powerful interpretive categories, lenses through which neglected nuances and complexities of Lynch's cinema come clear. Of course, it's very likely that Lynch's Gnostic atmospheres issue from Transcendental Meditation. After all, Transcendental Meditation is a highly eclectic "perennial philosophy" that shares key elements with Gnosticism: emphasis on an absolute but ungraspable principle of being, belief in the illusory nature of the material world, focus on immediate experience of the transcendent power, and hope that salvation comes through knowledge of the relationship between the individual soul and the ubiquitous principle of Being. However, these possible parallels are, in the end, immaterial. What is important is that the Gnostic situations presented in Lynch's films are, regardless of their source, capable of illuminating Lynch's films in ways they've never been enlightened before.

By now this point should be clear: none of these aforementioned films is simply *about* its respective Gnostic motif. Each movie *is* this religious situation, in form as well as content. Each picture fully inhabits the ambiguities of it spiritual predicament and ends up dwelling, however tenuously, in the gaps between clarity and confusion. In my mind, these qualities separate these films from Lynch's other four features. Obviously, Lynch's other feature-length films are replete with ironically religious elements. *Elephant Man* (1980) is clearly a Gnostic meditation on the transcendence of the gnarled body, and it meditates profoundly on the ironic interplay between ugliness and beauty, pain and redemption. Likewise, *Dune* (1984) is clearly about the growth of a messiah, and through its lurid dreaminess broods over the ambiguous relationships between development and destiny, enlightenment and violence. *Twin Peaks: Fire Walk with Me* (1992), though it appears to feature a dualistic struggle between good and evil, is really a weird fable of the inevitable interdependence between evil and good, transgression and charity. *The Straight Story* (1999), while it appears to be a transparently simple parable of the quest for redemption, is actually a deep contemplation of the complex connection between bitterness and generosity, the ridiculous and the authentic.

Still, while each of these films is an example of romantic irony, none, in my opinion, is as richly ironic as the films on which I focus. The difference is in degree, not in kind. All of Lynch's features are instances of transcendental irony; the five on which I focus just happen to be more sophisticated and robust in their uses of this kind of irony. In my mind, *Elephant Man, Dune, Twin Peaks: Fire Walk with Me,* and *The Straight Story* use irony in an occasional, even casual way. *Eraserhead, Blue Velvet, Wild at Heart, Lost Highway,* and *Mulholland Dr.* are organized by romantic irony to their very cores. The films are indeed masterpieces in this sort of ironic mode.

Treating commodities of commercial culture as if they are profoundly ironic vessels of religious experience sometimes feels dangerously silly. At the end of this chapter on the ironic religion of David Lynch, I wonder if I'm imbuing popular movies with depths and heights that aren't really there. The cause of this doubt is my re-watching of *Twin Peaks: Fire Walk with Me*, a movie that I still find to be, I'm ashamed to say, less interesting than Lynch's other films. What I see as the weak elements of this picture—including Lynch himself playing an FBI agent with a hearing problem—have made me begin to question my high estimate of Lynch's other work. If I am attributing nonexistent virtues to his idiosyncratic movies, then I am not only engaging in a ridiculous hermeneutical activity; I am also problematically vanquishing the essential distinction between good art and bad, profundity and superficiality. But I know where these thoughts will lead me—exactly where they have before: to another viewing of *Blue Velvet*. After once more watching this movie, I feel my doubts fade, and I am again convinced of the artistic genius of Lynch. This confidence, though, will once more dissolve. Again I will lie awake with vexing concerns over my own possible shallowness. And so I will once more take out *Blue Velvet*, or maybe *Mulholland Dr.* These are the troubles of romantic irony, and you never really know if the joke's on you or someone else, if you're stumbling on some path to salvation or just shuffling around in one place.

NOTES

1. The problem with watching this film on DVD instead of witnessing it as an art exhibition is this: one loses the texture of Lynch's screen. Still, watching the film is a strange, unsettling experience.

2. No significant work has yet been done on David Lynch as an important religious filmmaker. Nochimson in *Passion of David Lynch*, "Review of *Mulholland Drive*," *Film Quarterly* 56, no. 1 (Autumn 2002): 37–45, and "'All I Need is the Girl': The Life and Death of Creativity in *Mulholland Drive*," in *The Cinema of David Lynch: American Dreams, Nightmare Visions*, ed. Erica Sheen and Annette Davis (New York: Wallflower Press, 2004), 165–181, fruitfully discusses how Lynch's deployments of subconscious energies act to liberate characters from stifling social norms. While these works lay the ground for a study of Lynch's transformative art, they do not finally focus on Lynch and religion. John Alexander (*The Films of David Lynch* [London: Charles Letts, 1993]) helpfully argues that Lynch's films feature the alchemical motif of the nigredo—transformation through despair, suffering, darkness. However, Alexander doesn't focus on this transformation as a primary trend in Lynch's work. Jeff Johnson (*Pervert in the Pulpit: Morality in the*

Works of David Lynch [West Jefferson, NC: MacFarland, 2004]) rather reductively argues that Lynch, for all his ostensible weirdness, is an exponent of right-wing moral values. Of course, Johnson sorely misses Lynch's irony. Janet Preston ("Dantean Imagery in *Blue Velvet*," *Literature/ Film Quarterly* 18, no. 3 [1990]: 167–72) discovers ways that *Blue Velvet* is about religious motifs but doesn't argue that the film *is* religion.

3. Chris Gore, "David Lynch Interview: Is David Just a Little Weird?" *Film Threat*, January 17, 2000, http://www.filmthreat.com/Interviews.asp?Id=3.

4. David Breskin, "*The Rolling Stone* Interview with David Lynch," *Rolling Stone* 586 (September 6, 1990), quoted in Alexander, *Films of David Lynch*, 2.

5. Nochimson, *Passion of David Lynch*, 5.

6. Anne Persson, "Mr Lynch balanserar på gränsen," *Dagens Nyheter* (Stockholm), October 29, 1990, quoted in Alexander, *Films of David Lynch*, 13.

7. Richard B. Woodward, "Dark Lens on America." *New York Times Magazine*, January 15, 1990, 18–22, quoted in Alexander, *Films of David Lynch*, 7.

8. A similar description of these same ideas appears in Eric G. Wilson, *Secret Cinema: Gnostic Vision in Film* (New York: Continuum, 2006), 17–19.

9. Michael Bird, "Film as Hierophany," in *Religion in Film*, ed. John R. May and Michael Bird, (Knoxville: University of Tennessee Press, 1982), 10–11.

10. Ibid., 11–13.

11. Ibid., 14–17. Paul Schrader's idea of the transcendental film based on sparseness—as opposed to overabundance—is similar to Bird's notions (*Transcendental Style in Film: Ozu, Bresson, Dreyer* [New York: Da Capo, 1972]). It's significant, too, that Schrader uses Bresson and Dreyer—along with Ozu—to exemplify his ideas (1–15).

12. This idea runs counter to Schrader's notion that transcendental cinema is grounded on sparseness. I'm suggesting that overabundance can exhaust significance.

13. Friedrich Schlegel, *Philosophical Fragments*, trans. Peter Firchow (Minneapolis: University of Minnesota Press, 1991), 36.

14. Ibid., 45.

15. A version of these following passages on cinematic irony appears in Wilson, *Secret Cinema*, 21–24.

16. Rudolph Otto, *The Idea of the Holy: An Inquiry into the Non-Rational Factor in the Idea of the Divine and Its Relation to the Rational*, trans. John W. Harvey (Oxford: Oxford University Press, 1923), 11.

17. Ibid., 13–30.

18. Ibid., 63.

19. Immanuel Kant, *Critique of Judgment*, trans. Werner S. Pluhar (Indianapolis: Hackett, 1987), 244–47.

20. Ibid., 246, 252.

21. Friedrich Schiller, *Letters on the Aesthetic Education of Man*, trans. Reginald Snell (New York: Frederick Ungar, 1965), 64–68.

22. Ibid., 74–77, 79–80.

23. Cathleen Falsani, "Lynch: 'Bliss Is Our Nature,'" *Chicago Sun Times*, January 16, 2005, http://www.lynchnet.com/articles/suntimes.html.

24. Ibid.

25. Ibid.

26. Ibid.

27. Ibid.

28. This "Gnostic" context for reading five of Lynch's greatest films makes my book resemble—as I suggested in my preface—another: *The Passion of David Lynch*, by Martha P. Nochimson. Like Nochimson, I assume that Lynch's films embody a struggle between overly rationalistic (demiurgic) characters who attempt to reduce the world to their solipsistic will and more open, flexible (Gnostic) characters who transcend reason to gain an immediate, profound vision of the world's ambiguous, subconscious powers. At the same time, however, the "Gnostic" angle separates my study from Nochimson's. In focusing on Lynch's rebellions against reductive coherence and his embraces of liberating ambiguity, I am attuned to how his cinema connects romantic irony and religious experience. Focusing on this relationship, I am frequently led to questions, concerns, and conclusions that differ markedly from Nochimson's. For instance, my take on Lynch's irony leads me to conclude that Lynch's five great films end in irreducible duplicity. In contrast, Nochimson believes that these five films favor a fairly cogent, single vision. Likewise, my interpretations on the "rhetoric" of Lynch's five films encourage me to conclude that his cinema places viewers in the same position as protagonists: before an ambiguously "holy" event. This is not a strategy that Nochimson chooses to undertake. Finally, my interpretation of Lynch's five films in light of archetypal religious situations reveals a religious density in his films that is outside of Nochimson's more Jungian focus.

CHAPTER ONE

Eraserhead and the Ironic Gnosis

Dissecting a Cat

For Lynch, language is mostly an oppressive phenomenon, a procrustean system that rips objects from their mysteriously beautiful particularity and jams them into clearly labeled compartments. He expresses this view in an interview concerning *Eraserhead*. He admits in this conversation that he dissected a cat while making the movie. He was interested in the textures as models for the interior anatomy of the film's infamous baby. Gazing into the cat's innards, he claims, was an intense "experience," a tension between the sordidness of naming and the beauty of leaving things alone. To look on the dark, moist guts as functioning organs was to study something "pretty gross," but to witness these same glistening lumps as "isolated" entities was to perceive a "totally beautiful" event. "It's the kind of thing where," Lynch continues, "if you don't name it, it's beautiful. But as soon as you do, all kinds of associations become attached to it, and people will be turned off." In order to exemplify this point further, Lynch invokes a "piece of decaying meat." "If you happen upon it in a certain setting," Lynch states, "you could almost hear people *oohing* and *aahing* about its beauty. Until they knew what it was. Then they would not find it beautiful anymore. As soon as it had a name."[1]

Lynch's casual tone and shocking content hide a provocative theory on the relationship between perception and language. Lynch suggests that words tyrannize experience. They entrap seers into wispy ideas that have little to do with the actual world. They place barriers between eye and thing. They alienate subjects from objects. The only way to free oneself from this stultifying situation is to break beyond linguistic grids, to witness the world denuded of terms. With mediating filters gone, the cosmos will appear in all of its immediacy. It will arise before the sight as it is—as a series of strangely gorgeous happenings, a panorama of weird beauty.

Of course this is easier said than done, for it is almost impossible, if not entirely impossible, to perceive without conceiving. Ostensibly, the very structure of experience is linguistic. I can apparently only recognize the world through the lens of language. When I try to clear my mind of one set of words, another set instantaneously arises. I can't even think of thinking without words unless I use words to compose my thoughts. Language, it seems, is the true prison house. It reduces my potentially unique senses of the world to a lowest common semantic denominator. I can exist only in a dictionary, a vulgar lingua franca. I am living a life not my own. I am immured in a million terms.

Lynch appears to be aware of this situation, especially in *Eraserhead*. He realizes that words reduce us to a semantic status quo and that the only way to break beyond the linguistic given is to turn language back upon itself, to force it to consume itself. This is difficult (and ironic) labor, for it requires us to use words that immediately erase themselves and thus leave us hovering in an irreducibly ambiguous realm, a seemingly meaningless plane.[2] One way to achieve this difficult erasure and this subsequent release from clarity is to create a work of art that cancels itself by generating two diametrically opposed interpretations. This is Lynch's way of liberation in *Eraserhead*. He fashions a disturbing cinematic composition that contradicts itself at every turn, that constitutes a self-consuming artifice. At the end of the film, viewers are left in a hermeneutical limbo. They are compelled to face this possibility: linguistic meaninglessness is the most meaningful condition in the world. Hovering in this outlandish middle gap, audience members might, perhaps for the first time, begin to play—to take words seriously and as ridiculous jokes. Lynch's impulse to sever the conceptual shackles mooring the masses is Gnostic in spirit. Regardless of its variety, the Gnostic tradition shares one basic assumption: the physical world is a stifling illusion. Given this situation, the only way to free oneself into metaphysical reality is to reverse the conditions of the material plane. If language is the primary vehicle of signification in the realm of unreal matter, then the undoing of words is required for an escape to the real.

The problem, of course, is this: Gnosticism in any form is a mythological system that requires words for its very being. In this way, Gnosticism finds itself in a double bind: it is dependent upon the linguistic status quo that it wants to annihilate. How can one employ Gnostic critiques of oppressive materials without becoming fully a part of matter? Must a Gnostic necessarily prove the impossibility of Gnosticism?

To be a good Gnostic, it seems, is not to be a Gnostic at all. To avoid becoming immured by the weighty words of this physical world, the Gnostic must somehow posit his Gnostic beliefs while at the same time undercutting these very beliefs. He must simultaneously assert and erase his mythos. He must aggressively attack the conventions of the physical world; at the same time, he must question these very assaults.

This is exactly what Lynch attempts to do in *Eraserhead*. The film is replete with motifs from the primary Gnostic myths. It clearly loathes the muck and mire of the material world and longs to be free of sordid matter. It is especially disdainful toward the words that shackle the mind; therefore, it persistently searches for rifts in the linguistic system. But the movie also appears to be aware of the main problem of the Gnostic: he must use matter to critique matter, words to undercut language. In invoking the mythological systems of Gnosticism, the film makes itself dependent upon a complex grid of linguistic signification. Aware of this troubling fact, the movie works to undercut the very mythos that is its basis. In attempting to be Gnostic, it attacks gnosis. In espousing the annihilation of matter, it embraces the material.

Eraserhead attempts to erase the stultifying conventions of the recognizable world. To do this, it must erase itself, since it, too, is part of the very realm it wishes to wipe away. But this thoroughgoing consumption of stuff is not nihilistic. On the contrary, in becoming no-*thing*, not one particular thing or another, the film in the end turns to *no*-thing: the spiritual abyss transcending the horrific divisions of the fallen cosmos.

The Gnostic Vision

Gnosticism, which thrived in Alexandria and Rome in the first through the third centuries, was a wildly heterogeneous movement composed of numerous visionaries and sects. However, one idea ran through the various Gnostic visions: the physical world is an error, a mundane illusion covering the sacred truth of the transcendental realm. Though ancient Gnostics differed on how this error occurred and how to extricate oneself from this error, all believed that the Gnostic seeker should be persistently militant against the conventions of the material world, including the mainstream Jewish and Christian myths and the language systems constituting them. To speak unconsciously in the language of the day is to turn delusional; to strain the rules of the world's words with bizarre myths and fresh coinages is to challenge the oppressive diction and syntax and possibly to break beyond them.[3]

Of all of the Gnostic thinkers, Valentinus was the most subtle. He believed that matter enjoys no substantial existence at all but is instead a cosmic delusion issuing from a primal error. In order to escape the trammels of matter, all that one need do is to achieve a nonerroneous way of seeing. If one can achieve this, then what was thought to be solid and stable fades to naught, and one is free to merge with the transcendent. Of course, this conversion to correct seeing is easier said than done. This change requires nothing less than a total revolution in how one thinks and how one communicates.[4]

Let us turn briefly to the cosmology and psychology of Valentinus. This discussion of an ancient Gnostic way of liberation will clear ground for a reading of *Eraserhead* as a modern Gnostic myth. The system of Valentinus will be especially helpful when we consider the ironic double bind in which the film finds itself. In the beginning there was a perfect god, so perfect that it was beyond all perfection. Indeed, this god was beyond any human conception at all, including truth, beauty, and goodness. It was utterly mysterious, totally inaccessible, and fully hidden. However, at a certain point, this perfect god beyond perfection decided to create some companions. These companions were all particular manifestations of this god's various perfections. One companion exhibited its perfect thought; another, its perfect language; still another, its perfect wisdom. These numerous companions were called eternals. Each was purely spiritual and resplendent. Each entered into a gorgeous dance with the other companions. The perfect god was in the center. Around this god, his immortal friends danced. From their beautiful movements issued glorious music and shimmering light. This ravishing dance was all there was. All was good. No matter marred anything.[5]

However, at some point, the eternals decided that they wished to know their creator more intimately. They wanted to discover an accurate concept and a proper name for this being. What they didn't realize, though, was that this impulse was wrong from the start and thus doomed to fail. The creator was absolutely beyond conception and name, so any effort to conceive or to term him was inevitably on course for disaster. The eternals tried mightily to reduce the unbounded creator to a simple object they could know and name. Since the creator thrived beyond objectification, the eternals were unable to find the object for which they sought. They became terribly confused. This confusion grew into a fog. This fog after a time turned into an immense female body. This body became known as error. Unaware of her ignorance, error thought that she was perfect knowledge. So flush was she with her delusion, she imagined that she was a deity, the only deity. She set about doing what deities do: she created a world that she believed to be real. But this world is actually nothing but a vast error, a cosmic mistake. This world is also our own, a precipitation of spiritual misapprehension.[6]

This fall is psychological: matter, along with its qualities (ignorance and evil), issues from mental error. All beings born into error's universe—our universe—come to consciousness unaware that what they take for awareness of their environment is really forgetfulness of god. Each person reenacts the cosmic decline, mistaking ignorance for knowledge. However, like error herself, each individual is only a glance away from freedom. This glance would be gnosis, an intuition of these unnerving facts: to be puffed up with knowledge of the physical world is to suffer spiritual confusion; to flounder in worldly unknowing is to thrive in spiritual knowledge.[7] Such awareness would breed a keen paranoia toward the status quo, a refusal to conform to conventions of material knowledge. This awareness most especially would necessitate a rebellion against traditional ways of communication, an attempt to reverse semantic connections between words and concepts. It would inspire outlandish ways of expression—new symbols, new thoughts.

Valentinus attempts this rebellion against the status quo by overturning traditional Jewish and Christian theological concepts. He claims that the Judeo-Christian god is not omniscient and omnipotent but really mere error, a botched craftsperson capable only of making an insubstantial, and illusory cosmos. He further claims that Jesus is not the son of the Judeo-Christian father but instead the messenger of the perfect Gnostic deity beyond all earthly knowing.[8] These revisions of the theological given encourage aspiring Gnostics to question the conventions of society, to rise above the laws of the masses. If one undoes the rules of the fallen world, then he opens himself to union with the real god.

Valentinus's myth of potential redemption is of course extremely challenging. Even if the seeker tries to annihilate conventional ways of knowing and speaking, he must undertake his task while using the concepts and terms of the enemy. No matter how bizarre his expression, now matter how outré his thinking, he is constrained to the linguistic and conceptual system into which he has been thrown. His very Gnostic mythos, never mind its revisionary character, is contained by the grid. His only hope for escape is to turn his words against themselves, to consume his own artifice. Doing this, he will find himself extended into meaninglessness, into an indeterminate abyss. This abyss might well be no-*thing*, the mere annihilation of significance, but it might also be the *no*-thing, the hidden god existing before, above, and after all particular creations. If the abyss is the latter, then meaninglessness becomes the path to ultimate meaning, then conceptual confusion turns into the road to gnosis—immediate experience of the divine. Valentinus in the end doesn't aggressively challenge the linguistic status quo. Though his myths constitute conceptual rebellions, they are finally content simply to use the terms of the enemy. Still, his interpretations of the fall and redemption point to the linguistic problem. If the physical world is the erroneous creation of an ignorant deity, then any part of creation is tainted with illusion. The only way to escape the world's illusions is to find union with the transcendent god. This union can come about only through liberation from all the world's barriers. The last barrier is language, the very vehicle of our thoughts. To crack this barrier, one must become, essentially, mute and stupid, impervious to communication and understanding. Muteness toward the world is the hearing of the plenitude. Ignorance in relation to matter is intelligence of spirit.

Henry's Fall into Matter

Lynch's *Eraserhead* is a retelling of the basic Gnostic myth of the fall. The movie spends most of its frames depicting Henry's descent from an ethereal realm above space and time into a mundane plane designed by a wounded demiurge. Thrown down into this material realm, Henry (Jack Nance) is immediately shackled by unpleasant obligations generated by language. He tries to free himself through music: nonlinguistic communication.[9]

The film opens with a partly transparent version of a man's head floating above what looks like a planet. This suggests this man—whom we'll later know as Henry—initially enjoys a blissful condition beyond the sordid earth. The camera then tracks down to the planet and moves closely over its contours. This descent ends when the camera focuses on another man sitting and looking out of the window of a rundown old building. The man (Jack Fisk) is severely burned on one arm and on one side of his face. Before him are two levers. He pulls one lever and then another. The camera then moves to the apparent result of his pulls: a spermatozoon falls from the sky into a puddle of mud. The lens then seems to go down into the puddle and then to follow something out of the pit, through a portal, and into the white sky. The next thing we see is a man walking awkwardly through muddy vacant lots. It looks as though he is bewildered, unsure. It is as if he has just been born.

Lynch with extreme concision reveals the basic Gnostic myth of the fall. The soul of the man in the beginning hovers above the material world. However, the evil demiurge, scarred and squatting in the dark, uses his sinister technology to pull this ethereal soul down into matter.[10] This descent and entrapment is characterized by the imagery of birth. After the demiurge pulls his levers, the soul begins its fall and soon turns from a pellucid spirit into the opaque spermatozoon. This materialized "soul" then splashes into a putrid amniotic fluid in which it grows into a man. This man emerges from the womb of the earth into the harsh light of a burned-out industrial landscape.

The man—we don't yet know his name—features one of the strangest coiffures in film history. His hair is notoriously combed straight up and rises some five inches above his scalp. This elevated hair suggests that this man is in a state of surprised confusion, that he is never at home in any situation. This disorientation continues as he walks through dirty vacant lots surrounding emptied-out industrial buildings. As he treks cautiously over mounds of mud and slushy puddles—he at one point steps into one of these sloppy basins—he hears indistinct and annoying industrialized sounds. He also holds a weathered paper bag. He carries it cautiously, like he doesn't know what's in it. The man appears to have been thrown into a situation of which he knows nothing. Every step, it seems, takes him deeper into an unfamiliar and ugly landscape. It is as though he never knows where he is but simply finds himself strangely placed at each juncture.

He eventually wanders to a rundown apartment building. At this point, he seems surer of his actions. He might be getting used to the scene, more resigned to his new condition. He checks an empty mailbox. He enters into an old elevator and slowly ascends. He reaches his floor and trudges over to an apartment door. While he is unlocking his door, a strange, darkly attractive woman (Judith

Anna Roberts) appears in a doorway across the hall. Using the first words of the film, she tells the man that his girlfriend came by earlier and invited him to dinner with her family this very night. The man seems surprised by these remarks. He is not sure how to react. Ostensibly, he has forgotten that he even has a girlfriend. The woman's words appear to be calling him into a life of which he's not fully aware. Her terms indeed create the girlfriend as much as report her existence. They conjure up an entire set of obligations and responsibilities that immure the man further into this bizarre land in which he finds himself. The words, like prison bars, narrow his scope of activities and require him to perform deeds of which he'd otherwise be free.

The woman's words exemplify the way language primarily functions in *Eraserhead*. Words generally urge the man to do what he doesn't really want to do. They serve as indirect imperatives— you must do this, you must do that—and thus function as oppressive laws.[11] Though the man is already imprisoned in sordid matter and a prescripted life before the woman speaks, the words solidify and intensify his immurement. Before these sentences, he could at least move his body as he liked and anticipate surprise. After these remarks, he is constrained to a girlfriend, her family, and a dinner invitation. It seems as though the man has no choice in the matter. Without pausing to consider his options, he immediately makes ready to fulfill his obligation.

With a look of vague disgust—as if he's not looking forward to doing what he thinks he must do—he thanks the woman and walks into his apartment. Once inside, with the door closed behind him, he appears to feel more comfortable. The room has a warm, familiar feel. He plays a Fats Waller record on an old phonograph. He removes his wet socks and places them on a radiator. Then he remembers the words: he has a dinner date. He goes to his bureau and opens the top drawer. Among numerous scattered objects, he finds shards of paper. He places them together: they form the image of a woman, apparently his girlfriend. A jagged line runs through her face.

In these opening scenes, the basic contrasts of the film have been established with startling, and largely wordless, economy. On the one hand, there is the ethereal realm from which the man appears to have fallen. This realm is characterized by transparency and transcendence. The only space so far in the material realm that approaches this place is the man's apartment, where solacing music and intimate warmth protect the man from the climate outside. On the other hand, there is the material plane into which the man has declined. This environment is characterized by opacity and entrapment. It is pervaded by mucky, industrialized landscapes and words that impress into unpleasant duties. As the film develops, the former realm—the ethereal one—will be most fully exemplified by a strange woman singing in the man's radiator. The latter plane—the material one—will be most thoroughly instanced by a monstrous infant crying incessantly.

Making Conversation

This baby is announced for the first time during the man's dinner date with his girlfriend's family. The man—whose name, we soon learn, is Henry—again makes his way confusedly through the wasted landscape. He soon finds himself in front of a ramshackle house. The house is only feet away from a railroad track over which deafeningly loud trains run. Waiting for him by the door is an ordinary looking blonde-haired woman (Charlotte Stewart). She rudely accosts Henry, telling him that she didn't think he'd come. Henry sheepishly responds by saying that he didn't think she wanted him to.

This is the first of many such unpleasant scenes during this dinner occasion. The evening exemplifies the utter sordidness of the world into which Henry has fallen. First of all, the palpable material environment is disgusting. When Henry first enters the house, he notices a litter of seemingly innumerable puppies ravenously feeding at their mother's teats. The salad that he is expected to eat at the table is a gross mixture of anemic iceberg lettuce and an overabundance of sloppy salad dressing. The chicken served at dinner spurts viscid blood when Henry penetrates it with his carving knife.

The people in the house are also unseemly. The girlfriend sits awkwardly by while her mother (Jeanne Bates) drills Henry on his vocation; the girl then falls into an epileptic seizure assuaged only when her mother begins to brush her hair. The mother exhibits only two extremes of behavior. Most of the time she goes through her motions in a mechanical, zombielike way. Like an automaton, she interrogates Henry, brushes her daughter's hair, and makes the salad. However, after she witnesses the blood flowing from the chicken, she becomes a lust-filled maniac. She lets out a bacchanalian scream at the sight of the blood, and soon after she attempts to seduce Henry. The grandmother of the house (Jean Lange) is fully a zombie; she motionlessly and silently sits in the corner of the kitchen until the mother moves her limbs for her. The father (Allen Joseph), a plumber who must daily deal with waste-ridden water, likewise vacillates between mania and numbness. He is crazed with enthusiasm over the new, artificial chickens he is basting for dinner, and he inappropriately revels in the vapid clichés of banal conversation. But he is also half dead. He confesses that he can't cut the chicken because his arm is totally numb and he fears that he might cut himself. He is comatose while his wife lewdly bellows over the blood.[12]

The language used during the evening is likewise inappropriate. True communication seems impossible. After Henry enters the house, he sits uncomfortably on the couch. The mother launches into a series of entirely predictable questions; she seems programmed to "make conversation." Henry awkwardly responds to her inquiries; he seems unsure how to comport himself in this situation. The entire scene is a parody of the light banter that usually characterizes such occasions. The same strain of parody pervades the dinner table talk. The frenzied father expresses his excitement over the chickens before maniacally asking Henry to carve the birds. Henry is again unsure how to proceed. All he can do is express doubt over his ability to undertake this task. This parody of the "Rockwellesque" dinner scene is followed by yet another instance of parody. This time, the "serious" conversation about the suitor's intentions is mocked. After her outbreak of lust, the mother bluntly asks Henry if he and her daughter are having "sexual intercourse." The baffled Henry doesn't know how to respond. The mother then tells him that there's a baby at the hospital. Again, Henry is bewildered. It's as though he's hearing for the first time that such things as intercourse and infants exist. In this case as well as the other two, language does not convey meaning; it simply forces Henry to do things he doesn't want to do and strain to understand things that he doesn't quite get.[13]

The Monstrous Infant

Henry's neighbor told him that his girlfriend expected him for dinner. With her words, the girlfriend and her family essentially came into being for Henry. He appeared to have no awareness of them before the woman across the hall uttered these words. The same is true of the infant. The creature seems to arise into existence only after the mother mentions to Henry that there's a baby in the hospital. Before these words, Henry has no idea that he might be a father. Both instances show how words in the film make burdensome obligations, how they fashion phenomena that might otherwise not exist.

The infant of Henry and his girlfriend is one of Lynch's most notorious creations. It is a creature with a fishlike head that is hairless, slick, and disproportionately large. Two feet in length, its limbless body is shaped like a long, flat isosceles triangle. It is wrapped in white bandages. This monstrous being can do nothing but lie on a table with its head propped on an old, caseless pillow. It cries incessantly in a low, annoying whine.[14]

In the scene following the dinner party, Henry and his girlfriend find themselves in Henry's apartment. The girlfriend is attempting to feed the creature some sort of jellylike baby food. The infant keeps spitting the substance out. Henry looks on with a look of fear and confusion. He seems shocked to find this monster in his safe haven.

The appearance of this infant in Henry's apartment indeed suggests that almost nothing is exempt from the corruptions of matter. Henry's apartment earlier was a space in which he could escape the harsh climate and its oppressive utterances. It was a little realm in which he could sit silently in the warmth and listen to Fats Waller on his old phonograph. Now it is infected by matter in its lowest and most horrific form.

The infant as a fishlike creature recalls several archetypal symbols of the chaos of matter. It elicits the ocean, the primal slop in which the false god of the Gnostic wallows before he creates his ruined cosmos. It also intimates the great monster of this ocean, the Leviathan, the threatening whale. Finally, this freakish being suggests the cognates of Leviathan, both of which betoken matter at its most evil: the serpent and the dragon.[15]

This monstrosity makes Henry's life absolutely miserable. He is soon left alone with the infant after his girlfriend leaves in a huff over not being able to sleep. Henry spends most of his days and nights lying awake in his bed listening to the creature whine and cry. At one point, the infant becomes horrifically ill, infected with puss-ridden boils. Henry must labor to comfort the creature. He sits by its side with an old-fashioned humidifier bubbling nearby. Whenever he tries to leave the apartment even for a moment, the creature screams at the top of its perverse lungs, calling Henry back to its side.

The infant moreover appears to bring into Henry's life other monstrosities. Whether real or imagined—we can never tell which—these bizarre experiences suggest that this creature is more than a mere aberrant baby: it is a condensation of the terrors of the material world. One night after his girlfriend has returned, Henry awakens to her making sucking sounds and gnashing her teeth. While battling with her for the covers, he finds his bed infested with numerous wormlike creatures that resemble the infant in miniature. He throws these beings—which also resemble spermatozoa and small serpents—against his wall. One of them takes on life and begins to crawl up the wall. His very bed has become a place where snakes, matter at its worst, thrive.

On another occasion, after his girlfriend has once more disappeared, Henry is visited by the attractive woman from across the hall. Despite the baby's presence, she quickly seduces Henry. Immediately, Henry finds himself in bed kissing her. The bed, however, turns into a vat of white fluid, a viscous liquid in which he and the woman sink. At a certain point, all parts of Henry and the woman have sunk but the woman's bushy black hair. Her follicles float grotesquely on the surface of the fluid before going under. Soon after sinking through the vat, Henry finds himself on a cold and dark plane where the woman slinks in and out of the shadows. The look on her face is ominous, monstrous. Her presence suggests that sex in this world is nothing but perverse.

Not long after Henry has experienced this terror, he undergoes an even more horrific event. He finds himself in an old vaudevillian type theater apparently located in his radiator. There he meets a woman he has seen before in a dream or vision. She has oversized chipmunk cheeks, bright blonde hair, and a cloyingly innocent smile. She is generally bathed in light and thus appears to be a positive force. Just as Henry is on the verge of hugging her, she fades into the darkness. A single, leafless tree rolls out from the wings of the stage. Scared of this sign of his fallen state, Henry scurries to the corner of the stage. While dark blood flows from the base of the tree, Henry's head flies from his neck into the pool of blood. Where Henry's head was, now appears the monstrous head of the infant—the creature has infected the core of Henry's being. His head soon sinks through the bloody floor and lands with a splat on an abandoned street. A bum on a bench (John Monez) watches as a young boy (Thomas Coulson) retrieves the head and carries it to a pencil factory. A man (Hal Landon Jr.) drills out a portion of the brain and feeds it into a primitive machine. This machine transforms the gray matter into pencils with erasers. The pencil maker takes one of the pencils, makes a mark on a page, and then erases the mark. The ostensible owner of the factory then gives the boy some money for his trouble. Henry's brain has obviously been turned into inanimate matter, erased.

The Lady in the Radiator

The annihilation of the mark is especially significant in this film, for one of the few hopeful parts of Henry's life is his vocation as a printer. The erasure of this silent line—a wordless communiqué and thus a small rebellion against language—suggests that Henry's last possibility for liberation has been removed. One wonders at this point in the movie if there is any hope for Henry at all, or if he is to be forever immured in matter.

This erasure is the last of many dashings of Henry's efforts to extricate himself from the trappings of the material world. Henry's first attempt to escape his harsh environment involves music. As we have already seen, the film opens with Henry confusedly meandering through a sordid landscape of worn-down industrial buildings and muddy vacant lots. He retreats from these unseemly plots into the warm cocoon of his room. There he sits happily in front of his radiator and listens to the music of Fats Waller. The warmth of the radiator contrasts with the mucky cold of the outside, and the wordless tunes on his phonograph differ from the commanding words he will soon encounter.

We soon learn that Henry rebels against matter in other ways. At his girlfriend's dinner party, he reports to the mother that he is a printer. This suggests that his job requires him to copy down words and thus to participate in the language system that constrains his existence. However, Henry further reports to the mother that he's currently on vacation. This freedom from work is a rebellion. It shows that Henry is trying to liberate himself from the crass getting and spending of capitalism, from the commodification of otherwise autonomous beings into materials to be consumed.

Henry's most significant rebellion, though, appears to be psychological.[16] When the material world becomes especially oppressive, Henry envisions inside of his warm radiator the woman with the large cheeks, blonde hair, and kind eyes (Laurel Near). Whether this vision is real or a dream is immaterial. What's important is this: for Henry this woman signals a way out of the prison of matter. She is his Gnostic messenger, a bright presence from beyond who somehow exists secretly within the hidden corners of matter. She, through her wordless gestures and joyful songs, suggests to Henry that matter and its linguistic systems are stultifying illusions. She further intimates to Henry that only his silent and luminous soul is real and that this soul opens to a realm beyond confusion.

This woman first appears to Henry soon after his bed has become infested with worms that resemble spermatozoa and serpents. After Henry throws these vile creatures from his bed and watches one crawl up his wall, he notices his radiator light up from within. He gazes beyond the metal bars of this heating device and finds a small stage. The stage bulbs light up one by one to reveal the old vaudevillian proscenium. Carnival-like music from Fats Waller begins to play. In the center of the brightly lighted stage is the woman. She grins innocently, blissfully. She begins to dance slowly to the music. Under her feet are the same worms that Henry threw from his bed. Without ever losing her smile, she, in the midst of her dance, stomps on the worms. They squash bloodily under her feet. She obviously embodies a power greater than the material monsters that hound Henry.[17] The wordless music to which she dances transcends the oppressive language in which Henry finds himself thrown. Her dance itself destroys the monstrous symbols of the material prison in which Henry is incarcerated. In both cases, her presence shows Henry that the dark realm to which he finds himself shackled is not real but rather a nightmare from which he only needs to awaken. Once he does come awake, this realm will fall away as quickly as the tenuous veils of sleep. However, he is not yet ready to come to full consciousness. An instant after this vision, he is once again trapped in his room with the screaming monster baby.

Later in the film, Henry encounters this woman more intimately. After he kisses the attractive woman from across the hall and falls through his bed turned liquid, he actually finds himself on the stage with her. This increased intimacy suggests that there is a ratio at work: the more matter oppresses Henry, the more desperately he desires to know a way beyond the prison. At the point when he allows his lust to embroil him in a fluid-soaked sexual embrace, he longs to become one with the messenger who might free him from all material desire. Standing inches from her on the stage littered with dead worms, Henry watches her sing a heartbreakingly beautiful song about heaven. Though the song does feature words, it nonetheless points to a place beyond language: heaven. The lyrics to the song go like this:

> In Heaven, everything is fine.
> In Heaven, everything is fine.
> You've got your good things.
> And I've got mine.

After the woman finishes this song, she reaches gently toward Henry with a beckoning look in her eyes. She is inviting him to join her, to embrace her. Henry for once loses his confusion. With a determined look, he reaches toward this woman bathed in light.

However, just as he is on the verge of touching her, she fades into the distance, and the tree, the sign of Henry's fall into matter, rolls with a sinister squeak out onto the stage. Within minutes, Henry has lost his real head and had it replaced with the infant's monstrous poll. He is still not ready to escape the matter into which he has been thrown. On some level, he clearly still longs for the perverse security of his prison. Otherwise, he would be able to merge with the woman at this point.

Murdering Matter

Henry's rebellions against the material world are unsuccessful until he again experiences the lady in the radiator at the film's very end. Only at this juncture can he fully realize this: what most take for reality is fake, what most take for delusion is real. Once he understands this difficult reversal of the given, he can explode his material prison and dwell blissfully in the generous arms of the illuminated lady.

After the dream or vision during which his brain is transformed into a pencil, Henry finds himself back in his apartment alone with the monstrous infant. He is obviously more troubled than before. He paces nervously. At one point, he opens his door and looks across the hall. He is clearly interested in what's going on with the woman next door. It seems that he enjoyed his sexual experience with her earlier and is keen on another descent into lust. When he doesn't see this woman, he steps back into his hellish room. He appears to be desperate, disgusted. Then he hears voices outside his door. He checks to see who is talking. He discovers the woman from across the hall with another man. In the lurid light of the hall, the woman is no longer attractive. She leers at Henry and seems to mock him. Henry again retreats into his apartment. He sits down on his floor, weary and defeated. The baby emits a sound that appears to be laughter.

These two incidents push Henry to a deep hatred of matter. After once more wanting to act on his lust and then getting rejected, Henry likely falls into a state of guilt and self-loathing. Suffering this shame and remorse, the last thing he wants to hear is a monstrous infant laughing at him. Understandably, he's had enough of this world of gross desire and perverse fear. He can't take this place anymore. He wants out.

He decides, for once, to act. He will take revenge against this oppressive material realm. He finds a pair of scissors and walks over to the laughing infant. He begins to cut through the bandages covering its body. He quickly realizes that this bandage is the baby's skin—appearance has taken the place of reality. Underneath the white wrappings are moist and pulsating organs. Henry slowly stabs the scissors into what seems to be the monster's heart. The creature begins to spit up blood. It appears to be dying.

But the creature suddenly finds new energy. It expands into four times its normal size and rears up like a serpent on its coils. It has finally revealed its true identity—it is for sure the monster of matter's chaos, the serpent of sin and the dragon of destruction. It sways from side to side as if it is readying itself to strike. Henry recoils in terror. It seems as if he will now be consumed by matter once and for all. However, just when the monster is on the verge of lunging, the camera returns again to the planet that was hovering in the film's opening. The lens then moves to the burned demiurge and his deadly levers. This scarred creator is laboring to bring his creation back under his control. He violently pushes and pulls his levers. Gears grind and sparks fly. It's too late—in the next instant, the camera returns to the floating world to watch it explode into thousands of pieces. Henry's rebellion against matter has been successful. He has vanquished the illusions besetting him. He can now reascend to the real world from which he had fallen.

After the world explodes, Henry immediately finds himself facing the lady in the radiator. She is bathed in inviting light and smiling at him. Motes of luminous dust dance around Henry's head. He grins widely. He has transcended the illusions of matter and discovered the heaven where everything is fine.[18] The camera cuts to black. We then hear the same Fats Waller tune that Henry blissfully heard in his earthly apartment.

Erasing Salvation

These Gnostic elements are of course problematical, for they connect the film to a basic Gnostic mythology that is dependent upon the horrific world the myth wishes to vanquish. Even if the film valorizes silence and nonverbal communication, it nonetheless clearly manifests Gnostic motifs that are inextricably related to linguistic concepts. To see the film as an example of Gnostic myth is ultimately not to see it as Gnostic at all but as one more product of the demiurge, one more illusion in a plane of deception. Being overtly Gnostic, the film fails at Gnosticism.

How can the movie succeed as a Gnostic film? It can do this only by being Gnostic and not Gnostic at once, by laying out the Gnostic way of liberation and then immediately canceling this very way. Such an erasure of course leaves readers hovering in emptiness, in an abyss barely touched by conception. But this void need not be meaningless. It could well recall the great *no*-thing that is spirit, is life. If so, then negation is transcendence as well as annihilation, life as much as death.

The film achieves this thoroughgoing—and ironic—negation by literally erasing itself, by undercutting its Gnostic theme with counter-Gnostic elements. If from one angle the film is an attack on the ills of matter, then from another angle the movie is a paean to the vigor of material.[19] In a slightly altered perspective, every scene of Gnostic disgust turns into a site of organic vitality. Like a Rorschach blot or the "rabbit-duck" optical illusion, the film is both ascetic and sensual at once and thus neither antimaterial nor material. Spanning the spectrum of opposites, the movie is everything and nothing.

Let's return to the early moments of the film. Henry's head floating above a planet may not be the transcendent soul at all. Instead, this tenuous image might well suggest Henry's escapist dream, his inability to engage meaningfully with the vigorous material world. The head sinking down into the planet need not be a fall into sordid matter; this descent could be a depiction of a man waking up, sinking again into the realm of conscious aware-ness. If we take this latter reading seriously, then we can conclude that the burned man with the levers is not an evil demiurge but a figure of acute consciousness, a being burned by the vital fires of life, a guide from the realms of disembodied dreaming to fully fleshed regions of reality.

With these shifts in perspective in mind, we are prepared for a counterreading of the film, an interpretation that convincingly reveals the picture as an indictment of antimaterialist escapism and a celebration of matter's virility. In this view, Henry is not a brave Gnostic hero; he is a craven denier of sex. He is not a man legitimately pining for a reality beyond matter's illusions; he is one perversely trading robust reality for the wispy precincts of dream. He does not erase untruth. He rubs out natural desire.

Henry's early walk through the abandoned industrial landscape suggests that he is a man who needs to avoid people, someone afraid of human contact. He is understandably upset when the woman from across the hall reminds him of his girlfriend, of his connection to the human race. It appears that he is only happy when he can be alone in his dark apartment, a box blocking the sun. In this artificial sanctum, he surrounds himself with a totally fabricated environment, a space devoid of organicity. With his music, he shuts out the general din of the real. With his radiator, he enjoys unthreatening warmth. He is a man who wants to return to the womb, who hates the noonday glare. But this retreat from life is really death, enclosure in the tomb.

Even though he has ripped the picture of his girlfriend in half—a gesture renouncing her warm presence—Henry nonetheless drags himself to her house for dinner. He has not detached himself entirely from life's flows. However, regardless of his faint link to the organic, he still obviously hates material reality. His visit to his girlfriend indeed shows us the world through the eyes of an escapist, someone who finds the most ordinary temporal events to be hellish phenomena. For a printer on vacation—for a man who deals in artifice and who shirks work—the realities of labored existence will seem especially unseemly. In Henry's view, the girlfriend is an awkward epileptic who is overly reliant on her mother's nurturing. The mother of the girlfriend is an intrusive interviewer or a lusty harpy. The father, a plumber, is sullied by human waste; he is also inappropriately enamored of chickens. These people's environment is to Henry likewise disgusting. The nursing pups are grossly rapacious; the dinner salad is an unappealing slop; the chickens ooze horrific fluids.

The worst part of this grotesque scene, though, is the baby that emerges from it. In Henry's view, this creature resembles a monstrous phallus. It is a symbol of the sexual vigor that Henry lacks and of which he is afraid. Once this creature enters into his safe apartment, Henry becomes obsessed with sex. He guiltily desires it. He cravenly fears it. He wakes up in the night to find his girlfriend making lusty sucking sounds and to discover phallic worms infesting his bed. Unable to perform sexually himself, he imagines numerous little phalluses that might do the work for him. But he immediately recoils from his desire and throws the tiny penises violently against his wall. Then he envisions the woman in the radiator blithely stomping the worms. She is clearly an ideal for Henry—someone who is untroubled by sexual desire, who can easily destroy lust.

Soon after this sequence, Henry encounters the attractive woman from next door. He is very nervous around her, apparently afraid of her sexual advances. However, he soon yields to her lusty wiles and finds himself kissing her in a vat of milky liquid. Neither Henry nor the woman wears clothes. It seems as though Henry is on the verge of overcoming his aversion to sex when he and the woman sink into the milky substance. Immediately afterwards, Henry discovers himself on a dark plane. The woman emerges from the shadows. She is monstrously lascivious. Henry's guilt has once more gotten the best of him—he was unable to consummate his lust.

That Henry is ridden by guilt over his sexual desires is clearly borne out in the next series of scenes. After his attempted sexual encounter with the woman from across the hall, Henry finds himself face-to-face with the lady in the radiator. They are on the stage where she earlier crushed the worms. Deflated worm skins litter the stage. Once again, she is his ideal of chastity, a creature blithely unaware of lust. He wishes to hug her, to merge with her. However, before he can achieve this, the leafless tree rolls squeakily out from the wings. This tree recalls the tree of knowledge. It signals Henry's guilt over his lust and his impending punishment. Terrified, Henry cowers to one side of the stage and fidgets nervously with his fingers. Then he suffers his self-inflicted punishment. He becomes the infant, the oversized phallus that he desires and fears. Turning into a figure of pure lust, he loses his head, his reason. This part of his body descends into a bloody mire and splatters on an abandoned street. It is then transformed into a pencil, a phallus stiffened into a dead instrument, an implement meant to record the thoughts of the brain. This Cartesian nightmare captures perfectly Henry's greatest horror: that his overly rational head will become divorced from his utterly lusty body. If this were to happen, then he would have no control over his hated sexual desire.

Soon after this bizarre sequence, Henry once more finds himself trapped in his apartment. The infant persists in the corner. After Henry is rejected by the woman next door, the creature begins to taunt him. Disgusted again by his lust, Henry decides to take revenge on the phallic infant. He takes a pair of scissors, cuts the creature open, and stabs it between two organs that faintly resemble testicles. The creature violently rebels against this affront, but to no avail. Its wild death throes soon end, and Henry finds himself where he most wants to be—in the arms of the lady in the radiator, his figure of ideal chastity. In killing the infant, Henry has clearly castrated himself, divorced himself from the flows of life. Now he can live entirely in his dreams, utterly free of the vigor of the real. He can dwell comfortably in the safe radiator; he can rest in the bosom of sexless affection. He has returned to the womb, and there also found his tomb.

In proving itself to be anti-Gnostic—an indictment of sexual impotence—*Eraserhead* actually becomes fully Gnostic: an ironic erasure of the demiurge's semantics, an escape into the meaningless abyss, the holy void beyond the lucid illusions of the material world. Even though it undercuts its Gnostic mythology with a paean to organic energy, it in the end leaves viewers hovering in an interpretive limbo that recalls the pre-fallen condition, a state in which the cosmos is not yet divided into this and that, soul and body. Occupying the space emerging in the wake of cancelled oppositions, the film appears in the same light as a not-yet-named piece of rotting meat, as a thing not yet reduced to delusional human reason. Free of conception, the movie conceives gnosis, insight into the unhindered holiness of particularity, of energies liberated from mental enigma.

NOTES

1. Paul A. Woods, *Weirdsville, USA: The Obsessive Universe of David Lynch* (London: Plexus, 2000), 34.

2. John Alexander is attuned to this irreducible ambiguity. He writes that "*Eraserhead* isn't necessarily a film to make sense of in the way that it isn't necessary to make sense of an unsettling dream" (*The Films of David Lynch* [London: Charles Letts, 1993], 42). Chris Rodley helpfully recalls the initial responses to the film. He remembers that for early critics, attempting "an accurate or meaningful synthesis proved difficult. Downing blunt critical tools, [one] review concluded that *Eraserhead* was a movie 'to be experienced rather than explained'" (*Lynch on Lynch*, rev. ed. [New York: Faber & Faber, 2005], 54). K. George Godwin was an early critic who fell into this camp: he claimed that the "story" of *Eraserhead* "is couched in a collection of bizarre, seemingly meaningless images and inconclusive scenes which shatter the story's familiarity and make it frighteningly strange" ("Review of *Eraserhead*," *Film Quarterly* 39, no.1 [Autumn 1985]: 37).

3. I should be clear here that I'm using one of many specific interpretive modes in my description of Gnosticism. I'm using a strain of interpretation inaugurated by Hans Jonas in the middle of the twentieth century. This strain is existentialist, deeply influenced by Heidegger. This way of reading Gnosticism is especially illuminating for cinema (and literary) studies. Books on Gnosticism that more or less partake of this existential current are the following: Kurt Rudolph, *Gnosis: The Nature and History of Gnosticism* (San Francisco: HarperSanFrancisco, 1987); Jacques Lacarriere, *The Gnostics* (San Francisco: City Lights Press, 1989); and Ioan P. Couliano, *The Tree of Gnosis: Gnostic Mythology from Early Christianity to Modern Nihilism* (New York: HarperCollins, 1992). For a more historically based perspective on Gnosticism, see Elaine Pagels, *The Gnostic Gospels* (New York: Vintage, 1989). A more recent study that questions the validity of "Gnosticism" as a term is that of Michael Allen Williams, *Rethinking "Gnosticism": An Argument for Dismantling a Dubious Category* (Princeton, NJ: Princeton University Press, 1996).

4. In my discussion of Valentinus, I follow Hans Jonas, *The Gnostic Religion*, 3rd ed. (Boston: Beacon, 2001), 174–96.

5. This is a somewhat poetic embellishment of the opening of *Gospel of Truth*, probably by Valentinus. I base this account on the basic Gnostic myth of the unfallen spirit found in *The Secret Book according to John*. For *The Gospel of Truth*, see Bentley Layton, *The Gnostic Scriptures: Ancient Wisdom for the New Age* (New York: Doubleday, 1987), 253. For *The Secret Book according to John*, see Layton, *Gnostic Scriptures*, 29–35. See also Jonas, *Gnostic Religion*,179–81.

6. Layton, *Gnostic Scriptures*, 253–54. See also Jonas, *Gnostic Religion*, 174, 181–82.

7. Layton, *Gnostic Scriptures,* 255–56. See also Jonas, *Gnostic Religion,* 174–75.

8. Layton, *Gnostic Scriptures,* 254–55. See also Jonas, *Gnostic Religion,* 192, 194–97.

9. Martha P. Nochimson realizes this Gnostic entrapment: Henry, she writes, "becomes trapped" by the baby, "that labeled mass of matter, bound to it day and night, his only sense of freedom sparked by a dancing lady in a radiator who is simultaneously real and a dream" (*The Passion of David Lynch: Wild at Heart in Hollywood* [Austin: University of Texas Press, 1997], 151–52). Michel Chion more or less agrees, calling the lady in the radiator "an escape avenue from the hopeless hell of life on earth" (*David Lynch* [London: British Film Institute, 1995], 45). Alexander adds to these antimaterialist readings, concluding that the film is the story of a man "who wants no part" of "reproduction and birth" (*Films of David Lynch,* 42).

10. Alexander calls this burned man the "cosmic station master" (*Films of David Lynch,* 44).

11. Nochimson in her own way agrees, claiming that Henry is trapped in the "social machine of relationships" (*Passion of David Lynch,* 152). She further states that "the compulsions of labeling are the binding forces of the narrative" (153). For Kenneth Kaleta, Henry's great questions grow out of his bewilderment, his feeling of entrapment. According to Kaleta, the film persistently features Henry implicitly asking, "'Why was I born? Why am I living?'" (*David Lynch* [New York: Twayne, 1993], 17). Henry's great quest, Gnostic in spirit, is, Kaleta continues, "to master his own destiny" (ibid.). Jeff Johnson finds the film to be an all-out right-wing attack on the desire for material and the contemporary scene: he believes that the movie reveals "the dangers of premarital sex, unwanted pregnancy, mismatched marriage, and the economic and spiritual squalor of contemporary life in a wasteland of urban America" (*Pervert in the Pulpit: Morality in the Works of David Lynch* [West Jefferson, NC: MacFarland, 2004], 63).

12. Nochimson believes that these scenes reveal the "rigor mortis" of family (*Passion of David Lynch,* 156).

13. Chion highlights Henry's confusion in asking: "has [Henry] had sexual intercourse with Mary or not? For Mary has given birth to a baby, though she is not sure that this premature creature really is a baby" (*David Lynch,* 31).

14. Nochimson illuminates this relationship between the baby and language: "The 'baby' is the essence of illusion and reality—there is something there, but it is actually formless, held together only by the word and a bandage like swaddling. It is an ironic representation *not* in that it is the new life of the infant but rather the preclusion of new life by a social will" (*Passion of David Lynch,* 151).

15. Nochimson argues that the baby manifests the "chaos of energy within cultural pseudoforms"—that is, the infant embodies the web of tur-

bulent social forces that constrain Henry and turn him into a creature lacking any real volition (*Passion of David Lynch*, 156).

16. Chion indeed claims that "the world of the film is a mental world" (*David Lynch*, 30).

17. Nochimson remarks that the lady in the radiator is a "gift of [Henry's] subconscious and a means of contact with reality that is obscured by the threatening narrative growing around him" (*Passion of David Lynch*, 153).

18. Indeed, Nochimson claims that this lady is "pure light, incorporating air and electricity, two of Lynch's favorite images of living form" (*Passion of David Lynch*, 164). Chion to some extent agrees: the film in the end leaves us in "a beyond which is clearly designated . . . as a place where one never dies" (*David Lynch*, 46).

19. Chion makes this point. When Henry kills the baby, the "head tosses about with a mixture of cries of pain and rhythmic, patently sexual moans" (*David Lynch*, 33). This suggests that Henry's fear of the baby is the fear of sex. This is precisely George Godwin's point. (Godwin's essay is "Filming Lynch's *Eraserhead*," and it can be found in *Ciné-Fantastique* 4, nos. 4–5 [September 1984].) He claims (in the words of Chion) that the entire film is "placed under the sign of the fear of sex"; this means that the baby is a phallic symbol, and that the destruction of it is a "self-castration" (45). Alexander adds to this sensibility. He thinks that *Eraserhead* is a dream of "subconscious fears of becoming involved with the opposite sex"; these fears "create a 'worst possible' scenario of Kafkaesque proportions" (*Films of David Lynch*, 42). Godwin furthers this argument. He believes that the film is about how "the human mind, or intellect, or consciousness" has corrupted nature out of a desire to separate itself from nature and to control nature. However, this interference has made life "hostile" to man, "and this process has rebounded on him in the form of a perversion of one of life's most basic of forces: sex. The symbolic progress of the film reveals an ever deepening fear of sex . . . leading ultimately to a disgust which can only be remedied by a complete escape from it—into death" ("Filming Lynch's *Eraserhead*," 39). Each of these points bears out, in its own way, this reading: Henry is terrified of the vital energy that the baby embodies.

CHAPTER TWO

Blue Velvet and Paradoxical Chastity

The Play of Light and Dark

In an interview, Lynch once remarked on the subject of *Blue Velvet*. When asked about the film's ambiguous ending, he claimed that the main theme of this film is partial apprehension. Whenever we perceive things, he said, we quickly try to understand their mysteries. However, he continued, even though we might solve these mysteries to a degree, though we might half illuminate them, we soon realize that a part of them will always remain beyond comprehension, will stay in the dark. Hence, Lynch concluded, "there's always light and varying degrees of darkness."[1]

Hidden in these remarks is not only the movie's primary theme but also its main prescription: be open to the interplay between light and darkness.[2] Most of the film's characters—and most human beings—are on the side of either illumination or gloom. Those who seek only the darkness reduce everything around them to despair or evil. They become fixed in their sinister melancholia, as predictable as machines. Those devoted to the light are no better, for they flatten everything in their sight to happiness or goodness. They are addicted to untroubled joy and thus behave with the same predictability as their aberrantly woeful brethren. In both cases, people live only half-lives. They embrace one side of existence and repress, ignore, or forget the other. Doing so, they turn tyrants of experience, procrustean characters slicing away whatever doesn't fit their narrow desires.

How rare is the film character or actual individual who can break out of one-sided conceptions. This figure must somehow question the easy status quo of his culture, the comfortable "either/or" logic most people hold. He must eventually reject this divisive position and enter into unsafe realms of ambiguity and confusion, weirdness and turbulence. Though these regions are vexed, they ultimately are the only spaces in which one can gain fresh knowledge of self and world. Extended into the strangeness, one challenges his staid habits and stretches himself out into new terrain. In this terra incognita, he discovers heights and depths unavailable to those ensconced in safe havens.

Blue Velvet obviously shares with *Eraserhead* this emphasis on immediate experience over authoritative abstractions.[3] The latter film explores this focus in the context of Gnostic liberation from oppressive semantics. The former film, however, examines this emphasis from another angle: from the perspective of the blessed virgin, a perennial challenge to fixation and a perpetual invitation to flexibility. Traditionally, the female virgin has symbolized matter redeemed, physical presence untouched by lust for generation. As such, she has called into question views committed to earthly power and the laws that perpetuate this power. In countering this hunger for control and the institutions that support this control, this virginal character has opened her followers to pliable knowledge not fixed to one ideology or another, not hung up on this system of laws or that. This nimble knowledge is ultimately connected to beauty, to play: intense and vivid experience with little prefabricated purpose.

The Greek word for virgin, *parthenos*, suggests that the female can be chaste—free of material limitation—in two ways: either through having no sexual intercourse or through having sexual intercourse with many partners.[4] In either case, the virgin is unattached, not married to this man or that, everyone's lover or no one's. She can transcend matter though asceticism or sensuality, indifference to desire or exhaustion of desire. She can enjoy the decorous forms of civilization without becoming stiff; she can partake of the fecund flows of the wild without turning vulgar. She can play with forms without fixating on them. She can be, in the profound sense, ironic, able to take seriously the presences of the world while at the same time finding them inconsequential.

No wonder the *parthenos* has perennially been the object of male spiritual quests.[5] Hoping to die to matter and to be reborn in the spirit—to become free of material fixations and released into infinite possibility—men have sought to turn the virgin into an object of ascetic worship or sensual pleasure, into an icon or a lover. In either case, the goal is to know the virgin intimately, to gaze on her or to embrace her in hopes of achieving full acquaintance and appropriating her powers.

Lynch's Jeffrey Beaumont (Kyle MacLachlan), the protagonist of *Blue Velvet*, is on a quest for experience and knowledge. He undertakes this search through the agency of two women who approach the virginal archetype: Sandy (Laura Dern), an innocent high school girl not yet initiated into the mysteries of sex, and Dorothy (Isabella Rossellini), an experienced nightclub chanteuse practicing sadomasochistic sex with more than one partner.[6] Jeffrey hungers for what both have to offer—the possibility of liberation from the staid forms of "normal" behavior. Each woman in her complex duplicity shatters stifling conventions. Though Sandy is the wholesome "girl next door," she is obsessed with the sordid crime underworld. Even though Dorothy is the prototypical femme fatale, she is most moved by motherhood.[7] Paradoxically formed and formless, these virginal presences offer Jeffrey an ironic ideal: a set of values that erases itself, purity that is corrupt, order dissolving into chaos.

Lynch's cinematic forms in this film correspond to these ironic female icons. Lynch persistently presents images that assert and deny meaning, that constitute shimmering pictures and insignificant blanks. Like the mythical *parthenos*, his sequences might fixate ascetically on one pristine idea and they might flit wantonly around more concepts than the mind can hold. In the end, it is impossible to tell, to settle on whether his scenes are serious or in jest. Witnessing these self-consuming forms, the viewer finds himself in the same place as the film's protagonist, confused before visions that might offer liberating experience, or that might fade like phantoms.

Lynch indeed appears to realize that the transcendental mode of the blessed virgin requires the same erasures as the Gnostic method of liberation. He seems to know this: a fixation on the ideal of the blessed virgin ultimately goes against the ideal of the blessed virgin. To get hung up on a static system of spiritual freedom is in the end to give over to oppression. The only way to find true virginal emancipation is to question the very value of virginity, to embrace transcendental chastity while at the same time denying it. This is the secret of Lynch's unsettling forms in *Blue Velvet*. He clearly espouses the ideal of the blessed virgin and thus presents his female characters as icons of spiritual liberation. But at the same time, he questions the efficacy of the virginal presence and therefore features the women in his film as failed icons. But in erasing the virginal power, he actually (and ironically) lauds it. In annihilating the image of the virgin, he shows a commitment to the virgin's greatest potency: her ability to free her devotees from the tyranny of reductive thinking, from the flattening of ambiguity to one stable idea.

The Blessed Virgin

The Catholic tradition, ecstatic on the Mother Mary, inflects chastity as a sexless state—to avoid sexual intercourse is to be a virgin. The Greco-Roman pagan tradition, finding purity in the sexually active Athena as well as in the sexually dormant Artemis, offers an alternative version of chastity as indifferent promiscuity: the liberation from sex through the purgation of sex.[8] Throbbing between these two versions of the *parthenos*—*parthenos* Mary, Athena *parthenos*—is a certain current in the Gnostic tradition that casts the virgin as the prostitute, the whore as holy. In pausing on this trend, I want to unmoor chastity from its typical semantic context—the avoidance of sexual intercourse—and release this idea into more appropriate and complex significations. Doing so, I hope to discover a powerful lens for illuminating the mysterious female presences in *Blue Velvet*.

A classical version of the Gnostic myth can be found in *The Secret Book according to John* (c. 180 AD). For the author of this work, the origin of life is not the God of the Bible but a radically transcendent power. Out of this original mystery emanates androgynous *aeons*. This source and its outflows compose the *pleroma*, the plenitude. However, one of these *aeons*, Sophia, disrupts the harmony and produces Ialtobaoth. He stupidly believes he is the only god and fashions a cosmos poorly modeled on the *pleroma*. This universe is our own. Penitent, Sophia persuades the eternals to let her descend into matter to plant a divine spark (*pneuma*) in humans suffering in the corruption. She casts off her spiritual purity and takes on polluted form, the shape of the serpent. In this guise, she ascends to the top of a tree and seduces Eve and Adam into eating the fruit of knowledge. When the two consume this fruit, they experience within their breasts the birth of spirit and the advent of gnosis. They realize their origin in the *pleroma* and their exile in this world. They vow to reject the laws of Ialtobaoth.[9]

This basic myth is the beginning of the double life of Sophia. Even though she descends into the material realm to rectify her error, a part of her remains in the *pleroma*. Indeed, her spiritual side is inseparable from the most pristine presences in the plenitude. But this eternal identity remains only half of her existence. Once she descends into time in hopes of redeeming Adam and Eve, she stays on the material plane to take on yet other physical forms and to call home still other exiled creatures.[10] Though she thrives in the unsullied air of eternity, she is willing to take on any identity in order to awaken in Ialtobaoth's slaves a spiritual yearning. She will turn snake, criminal, and prostitute. This is her blessing and her curse. As a savior of all humankind, she is a material form unattached to the ills of matter, a virginal presence. As the guilty cause of the first error, she is made to suffer the most degrading elements of the fallen world, to become a whore.

Sophia's double life is connected to the related myth of the Gnostic Helena, another virgin in eternity and prostitute in time. According to Irenaeus, Simon Magus, one of the first Gnostic figures, traveled around with a prostitute named Helena. Simon claimed that this harlot was none other than the "first thought" (*ennoia*) of the hidden god and hence the mother of all life. Apparently, this thought at one point descended into impure regions below her eternal origin and there created angels and other manifestations of divine power. These beings proceeded to create a world of their own—our material world—and, out of envy, imprisoned Helena in this world. Over centuries, Helena transferred her spirit from body to body in hopes of finding a way out of her captivity. She finally found herself entrapped in the flesh of a prostitute. Languishing in a brothel, she was discovered by Simon. Unbeknownst to her, Simon had been sent by the hidden god to redeem the first thought. Simon liberated this spirit by reminding her of her true identity. Then, he and Helena together became itinerant redeemers. They traveled from town to town telling people to reject the creation of Jehovah and to break his laws.[11] Their message was libertine: transcend matter through spontaneous actions, through indifference to all boundaries.[12]

Like Sophia, Helena combines both modes of chastity. She is a pure manifestation of spirit and thus fundamentally untouched by matter. She is a sullied inmate of the material realm but indifferent to moral laws and physical limitations. In either case she is free, capable of dwelling in the world without taking it seriously, able to be present and absent at the same time. For this reason, she proves an ideal redeemer for those souls aching under the oppressive strictures of the status quo. Through example and word, she teaches aspiring Gnostics how to dwell in time while thriving in eternity.

The figures of Sophia and Helena alike clearly practice a sort of transcendental irony. They are trapped in physical forms but identify with formless spirit. They are spirits connected to eternity but take seriously the work of redeeming creatures trapped in time. From the perspective of eternity, they remain untouched by bodies; thus, they play with the elements of the creation. From the angle of time, they are the only hope for liberation; hence, they embrace the things of the universe.

Shimmering Curtains

Blue Velvet begins with a beautiful image that proves the ideal toward which Jeffery and the film itself appear to strive. Waving

sinuously behind the opening credits, almost in rhythm with
Angelo Badalamenti's haunting score, is a curtain of blue velvet.
The rustling tapestry resembles a shimmering ocean. As it oscil-
lates between crest and trough, it reflects light into an exquisite
dance of colors: white and silver, sky blue, royal blue, navy blue,
and then again the silver and white. Dancing, the curtain seems
actually to breathe, as if it were organic, sentient.[13] Like an ocean
or a living thing, the velvet gathers pattern and turbulence, darkness and light. In placing these oppositions into fruitful relationships, in throbbing between quivering blackness and blinding
white, the curtain figures the structure of the *parthenos*—form
and formlessness, crystallization and chaos. Beginning with this
image, Lynch places the audience in anticipation. Will the film
achieve this balance, or will it either sink into ooze or freeze into
frigid order?

Lynch addresses this question in his favorite mode: irony. The
film proper opens on bright red roses wavering in front of a white
picket fence. They are luminous, gorgeous. However, the rose and
fence are famously saturated with light and perhaps a little too
perfect—they look artificial, unreal.[14] The next shot rather clearly
heightens the unreality. A vivid red fire truck moves down a
quaint neighborhood street in slow motion; a smiling fireman
waves. This shot is followed by a return to a white fence, this time
serving as a background to yellow tulips. We then see children
crossing a quiet street under the tender guidance of a crossing
guard, again in slow motion. These bright reveries unfold to the
music of Bobby Vinton singing his 1963 hit, "Blue Velvet." His
voice recalls the popular crooners of the forties and fifties, the
sentimental music of ideal America: small-town neighborhoods
manicured by responsible citizens and protected by a benevolent
government. The camera then focuses on a man watering a well-
kept backyard. He wears clothes that recall the forties or the fifties.
Inside, a woman who is apparently his wife sips coffee in a living
room whose décor likewise recalls mid-century America. The
expression on her face is complacent. She and her husband resemble characters from a forties film of Frank Capra or a saccharine
domestic sit-com of the fifties. These characters and their environment constitute an ironic version of the "good life," suggesting

that most people envision happiness merely as banal comfort, a condition from which all messiness has been expunged, all evil. This is the Hollywood Eden, a repression of turbulent energy in favor of prefabricated order.

Because the denizens of this world are unaware of polarity—the interdependent relationship between chaos and order, darkness and light—they are stunned when turbulence erupts into their studio existence. Crime and death to these ciphers of Hollywood are purely fictional, dreams that cannot touch them. The wife while serenely drinking her coffee watches a black-and-white crime drama, likely an old film noir. The pistol glimmering on the screen does not affect her in the least—the sordid noir world is to her a matter of television. The husband contentedly watering his lawn seems shocked and becomes irate when his hose gets tangled. Unused to accidents, he becomes so angry that he suffers a heart attack or a stroke. He falls to the ground and writhes in the mud created by the overabundant flow of hose water. As he loses consciousness in the muck, a thirsty neighborhood dog continually jumps up to bite the geyser. The camera slowly moves from this absurd scene to the grass and then under the green surface. Deep in the dirt, a colony of black beetles appears. In a horrifying close-up, these beetles squirm all over one another. They produce a terrifying sound, a mix of flowing lava and ravenous crunching. Because the Hollywood Eden represses and demonizes this subterranean realm, when it does erupt—in the form of violence or death—then it appears not as the necessary other of the sunny plane but as a hell, a cauldron of liquid brutality.

This is what happens when one divides a bipolar cosmos of mutually inclusive oppositions into a hierarchical universe of mutually exclusive antinomies. What is in reality a thriving rhythm of interdependent polarity, a crepuscular dance of darkness and light, becomes in perception a dualistic battle between good and evil. To sever energy from form and favor form over energy is to create a world in which form is valued as the only good and energy is demeaned to evil. Having repressed turbulence, the Hollywood Eden turns into a static husk opposed to all that is dynamic and unpredictable. When the darker forces break into this shell, they appear not as vigorous currents but as devilish pollutions. In this way, "good" society sabotages itself, dooms itself to vague paranoia, chronic xenophobia, quiet desperation. To live a vital existence, one must shatter the shells of Hollywood and search for the interface between oppositions. When one discovers this overlap, one can draw virtues from energy and form, matter and spirit, without being limited by either pole. This is the liberation of virginity.

Unlike his father (Jack Harvey), who in his rigid shell of convention is undone by turbulence, Jeffrey is open to the boundary between darkness and light, eager to gain knowledge and experience beyond the bifurcating codes that have shaped his life so far. His very name—a combination of "peace" and "beautiful mountain"—expresses his quest: to transcend the comfort of the status quo to the heights of vision. Aptly, the first shot of Jeffrey features him walking through a vacant lot on which stands an abandoned shack. The lot serves as a path between Jeffrey's manicured neighborhood and the hospital where his father recovers. This *mise en scène* figures Jeffrey's hunger for spaces forgotten by the mainstream, regions that take him across from one level to another. When Jeffrey reaches his father at the hospital, he is shocked at what he finds, awakened to a new way of seeing. Hooked to numerous monitoring devices, his father looks less like a human and more like a machine. When the older man attempts to speak, he is unable to move his mouth. An expression of horror wrenches his face. Jeffrey is stunned. His lawgiver and role model, his exemplar for the status quo, is now moribund, mute, and terrified. This fall of the father forces Jeffrey to find his own codes and conventions. It also opens to Jeffrey a world of unspeakable mystery, frightening conundrums reducing grown men to tears. Jeffrey does not flinch before these bracing possibilities. On his way home, he again crosses the vacant lot. As he picks up pebbles to throw at a bottle near the abandoned shack, he notoriously finds a severed ear, rotted and teeming with ants. Instead of recoiling at this grotesque sight, Jeffrey without hesitation gathers the ear in a bag and takes it to the police headquarters.[15]

In the police station, Jeffrey once more faces an obstacle to his quest to discover the densities of experience on his own. There he meets Detective Williams (George Dickerson), a man from his

neighborhood and the father of a daughter named Sandy. Williams's
detached delivery suggests that the law is aloof to lived experience,
that it is ultimately indifferent to strangeness. Facing such indifference, Jeffrey could easily assume that his discovery is uninteresting and thus negligible. He could quickly decide to give up his
hope of solving the ear's mystery. However, he rejects Williams's
hard-boiled insensitivity in the same way that he avoids his
father's clichéd behavior. In both cases, Jeffrey proves himself
capable of seeking fresh experience, of following his own path
toward weird knowledge.[16]

This ear, true to its anatomy, obviously serves as a threshold, a
portal between outside and inside, light and dark, apparent and
hidden. From the minute Jeffrey encounters this detached organ,
he is pulled into an unfamiliar underworld, both a psychological
disposition attuned to turbulence and an actual world fraught
with violence and death. If Jeffrey's world before he discovers the
ear resembles the cinematic environs of Capra, then the world he
inhabits after finding this detached organ is close, as many have
noticed, to the brutal noir cityscapes of, say, John Huston.[17] The
scene following the one in which Jeffrey deposits the ear with the
detective is a telling modern instance of the noir genre. The camera shows a dark stairwell leading up to a single room. The door
to the room opens. Standing at the threshold is the shadow of a
man. The shadow moves out of the lighted portal and descends
into the darkness. When this dark figure reaches the bottom of the
stairs and returns to the light, its identity is revealed—it is Jeffrey.
He tells his mother (Priscilla Pointer) and aunt (Frances Bay) that
he wishes to go for a walk, even though it's dark outside. Though
he makes his way down familiar sidewalks—the same byways that
glimmered earlier in the tawdry light of the American dream—he
experiences these paths in a different way. He first notices not a
smiling fireman or crossing guard but a sullen fat man standing
with his small dog. The man glowers at Jeffrey through dark
glasses. Making his way past this presence, Jeffrey looks down the
tree-lined lane. The trees are gnarled and dark, making the neighborhood street look like a spooky forest. Jeffrey looks up into the
branches. They wave eerily in the wind. Unsettled, Jeffrey remembers the ear. As the organ moves closer to his mind's eye, a sinister

hum pervades his head, as if a resounding chasm descends under the ear's opening. His mental gaze approaches even closer and then appears to go through the portal into the darkness below. The sound intensifies. Jeffrey's interior eye has entered into a realm beyond visual representation, an abyss of unknown energies. He will need a guide if he is going to negotiate successfully these unmapped realms. Luckily for him, he immediately encounters two virginal forms who can lead him through the darkness.

Sandy and Dorothy

Throughout the film, Jeffrey vacillates between the old world of soda pop complacency and a new one filled with violent obsessions, between small-town melodrama and big-city noir.[18] These two poles are figured by the two women in his life, Sandy and Dorothy. Jeffrey's goal, it appears, is to find a rapprochement between the bright world of Sandy and the dark one of Dorothy. If he can overcome the dualism of the status quo, he might be able to discover how Sandy's world of law and spirit is dependent upon matter (Sandy means "sand," "dirt," "earth") and how Dorothy's environment of criminality and lust requires spirit (Dorothy signifies "gift of god").[19] He might understand the mystery of virginity, the vexed interpenetration of spirit and matter, form and formlessness.[20] This understanding, once attained, might liberate him into the ironic vision, an ability to unmoor structure from signification, signified from sign. This undoing, though potentially confusing, might free him from fixation on limiting conventions and open him into fresh and seemingly infinite possibilities for being. Material forms would become portals to invisible vistas; ambiguous scenes would cohere into definite directions.[21]

Sandy first appears in the midst of Jeffrey's nocturnal walk. After envisioning the ear dissolve into a humming abyss, Jeffrey visits Williams to ask if the detective knows anything more about the ear. Williams stays tight-lipped and sends Jeffrey home with no answers. As Jeffrey makes his way down the walk in front of the Williams residence, he hears a disembodied voice asking, "Are you the one who found the ear?" He looks toward the voice and sees only a dark willow tree rustling in the wind. Out of the blackness emerges a shadow that slowly coheres into a mysterious blond-haired woman. She says, "Are you the one who knows about the ear?" Jeffrey asks her how she heard about the ear. She responds, "I just know." But this noirish apparition, recalling the twilight ghostliness of such femme fatales as Joan Bennett, quickly transforms into a wholesome teeny-bopper hungry for a zany caper. The woman is Sandy, Williams's daughter and a senior in high school. As she and Jeffrey meander down the sidewalk, they move between teenage flirting and discussion about the ear. Sandy tells Jeffrey that she has overheard her father's conversations on the case of the ear and has gathered that a woman named Dorothy Vallens is involved. She leads Jeffrey to Dorothy's apartment building. Meditating on the unseen woman dwelling in this structure, Jeffrey rhetorically asks, "It's a strange world, isn't it?"

This initial conversation between Jeffrey and Sandy epitomizes their relationship. On the one hand, Sandy is the "girl next door," the "prom queen," the pure virgin. Like a high school girl from a television show or film of the forties and fifties, she spends her days mooning over boys, giggling with her girlfriends, and hanging out at the soda shop. Jeffrey, a graduate from Sandy's high school home from college to tend the family hardware store during his dad's illness, readily enters into this teeny-bopper scene. He speaks with Sandy in a "gee-whiz" high school lingo, flirts with her as if he is reading a script from *Father Knows Best*, and courts her in a large fifties red convertible. But on the other hand, Sandy, despite her wholesome appearance, is Jeffrey's initial guide into the noir world. Appearing from the sinister darkness, she provides Jeffrey the first clue to his investigation of the crimes surrounding the ear. Drawn to gloom as much as brightness, she leads Jeffrey to the "bad" side of town to see Dorothy's apartment building. These subterranean qualities of Sandy attract Jeffrey as much as her overt ones. Her invitation into the corridors of real crime not only prompts Jeffrey's realization that the world is "strange." It also inspires him to go on a quest to solve the riddle of the ear, an outward journey toward factual knowledge and an inward pilgrimage toward self-awareness. Seducing Jeffrey toward these uncharted realms, Sandy performs the function of the archetypal virgin—a site of liberation from fixity, of birth unhampered by matter.

After intensifying Jeffrey's growing curiosity, Sandy becomes fully complicit in his investigation. The day after their first meeting, Jeffrey picks up Sandy from high school and takes her to a soda shop. There, in the midst of banter reminiscent of *Happy Days*,[22] Jeffrey prepares Sandy for his quest by telling her that there exist "opportunities in life for gaining knowledge and experience." In seizing these opportunities, he continues, "it's sometimes necessary to take a risk." In this case, Jeffrey concludes, one must "break the law" in order to undergo these fresh experiences and insights. Sandy agrees to hear his plan. Jeffrey will disguise himself as an exterminator to achieve entry to Dorothy's apartment. While he pretends to spray, Sandy will distract Dorothy by knocking on her door and pretending to be a Jehovah's Witness. During the time that Sandy talks to Dorothy, Jeffrey will jimmy a window so that he can later break into the apartment. Once inside, he will "hide and observe." Sandy responds by saying that this plan is a "good daydream" but in reality is dangerous and weird.

Sandy's words aptly detail the two-fold nature of Jeffrey's scheme. Measured against the conventions of wholesome small-town "reality," Jeffrey's plan is dreamy, a suspension of normal logic, an entry into an unpredictable outland. Hungry for this alternative world, the dream is very likely to be dangerous and weird. In order to realize this reverie, Jeffrey must break several laws—he must impersonate an exterminator, break into a private residence, and voyeuristically watch the movements of a stranger. But as Jeffrey is beginning to realize, these are the sacrifices required for the transcendence of the stifling codes of the status quo. Sandy senses this insight herself. She in the end agrees to help Jeffrey carry out his plan.

In undertaking this design, Jeffrey first meets Dorothy. To reach her apartment, he must enter into a building called "Deep River Apartments," a name suggesting profound currents. Yet, even as Jeffrey sinks into the dissolving flood, he rises. Dorothy's apartment is on the seventh floor. As Jeffrey struggles up the steep flights while carrying his equipment, we recall that "seven" figures completeness—seven planets in the solar system, seven days in a week. This is the logic of Jeffrey's quest—he must sink to ascend,

gather opposites to find the dynamic middle.[23] Dorothy's apartment embodies this duplicity. Her living room is carpeted and
furnished in dark purple. This room ends abruptly at the kitchen,
tiled and painted in bright white. While Jeffrey moves through
this two-fold realm spraying, he finds a key to Dorothy's apartment and puts it in his pocket. When he returns to her house later
that night, he finds that Dorothy, too, is a virginal mixture of matter and spirit—violent desire and charitable longing.

While the sultry Dorothy is singing at a nightclub, Jeffrey and
Sandy drive to her building. As Jeffrey departs for the apartment,
Sandy captures his duplicitous condition when she wonders aloud
whether he is a "detective or a pervert." He of course is both—a
man questing for hidden truths revealed beyond the conventions
of the public morality. Jeffrey illegally enters Dorothy's apartment. Safely hidden in the closet when she arrives, he witnesses
her talk on the phone with someone who ostensibly has her husband, Don, and child, Donnie, held captive. Though she is
allowed to speak briefly to Don, she spends most of the short conversation talking to the apparent kidnapper, who requires her to
call him "sir" and also to say to him, "Mommy loves you." When
she hangs up, she weeps on the floor before retiring to the bathroom. She comes back to the living room wearing a blue velvet
robe that recalls the shimmering cloth from the film's beginning.
Her double garb—dark cloth and white reflection—provides a
fitting transition to her subsequent gestures, radical departures
from the maternal concern she has shown for her child. Dorothy
overhears Jeffrey in the closet. She grabs a knife, opens the closet
door, and forces Jeffrey to emerge into the living room. She makes
him undress and nicks his face with her knife, all the while commanding him not to look at her. But she turns from violence to
lust. She begins kissing the naked Jeffrey near his penis.

Dorothy's vacillation between traditional "family" values and
aberrant sexual desire continues. She and Jeffrey are interrupted
when someone knocks. Dorothy sends Jeffrey back to the closet
before letting in Frank Booth (Dennis Hopper). Frank, dressed in
black, takes on the violently dictatorial persona that Dorothy used
in relation to Jeffrey, while Dorothy plays the submissive role Jeffrey enacted in connection to her. While he sips whisky that

Dorothy has brought him, Frank directs her to open her robe and spread her legs. He commands her not to look at him. He then inhales vigorously from a small nitrous oxide cylinder attached to his belt. He approaches Dorothy and begins to intone, "Baby wants to fuck." Dorothy responds, "Mommy loves you." Frank hits Dorothy in the face, again ordering her not to look at him. Dorothy moans with pleasure. Kneeling in front of Dorothy's exposed crotch, Frank says, "Baby wants blue velvet." Dorothy places part of her robe in his mouth. He puts another part in hers. He then throws her on the floor and rapes her with his fingers. He then simulates sexual intercourse until he reaches orgasm. Dorothy seems to be experiencing keen pleasure. As Frank gets up, he again hits Dorothy, telling her not to look at him. He blows out the candle, says for a second time, "Now it's dark." He reminds Dorothy that she must stay alive for the sake of "Van Gogh" and then leaves.

From the closet, Jeffrey has witnessed this bizarre scene of sadistic, masochistic sex mixed with incestuous role-playing—Dorothy pretending to be a mother and a daughter, Frank acting out the son and the father. (Many have indeed noticed the Freudian elements of this scene: Jeffrey like a child has beheld the primal scene—sex between his parents. This sight of course leads to Oedipal tensions.[24]) Though Dorothy and Frank are obviously consumed by "perverted" lusts, they are also hungry, however awkwardly, for traditional "family" values. After Frank leaves, Dorothy tries to bring Jeffrey into this strange domestic configuration. She at first tenderly seduces him. While Jeffrey is caressing her exposed breast, Dorothy requests that he hit her. She wishes for him to play Frank, to become father, husband, and son so that she can turn into daughter, wife, and mother. She is inviting him to join a new family, a dark counter to his daytime domestic situation. Jeffrey is not ready for the disturbing underside of the virginal presence: the liberation from earthly desire through the exhaustion of desire. He recoils in horror and leaves the apartment.

The Realms of Law

Through the agency of Sandy and Dorothy alike, Jeffrey for the first time faces the terror of turbulent realms beyond his ordinary

knowledge and experience. After his discovery of the ear awakened him to possibilities beyond his familiar scene, Jeffrey allowed
himself to be led by these two virginal presences to the strangeness of the world and his own heart. Now, still with these female
forms guiding him, he encounters firsthand the violent weirdness
of Frank and to his surprise finds that he possesses the same aberrant yearnings in his own breast. While this discovery frightens
him, it also offers him possibilities for expanded experience and
knowledge that might empower him to become virginal himself,
to turn innocent, ironic—to care and not to care.

Frank embodies unbridled chaos untinctured by Sandy's
ambiguous wholesomeness and Dorothy's misplaced love. Beyond
the oppositions embodied by these virginal figures—conflicts
between matter and spirit, lust and love—Frank blurs all meaningful distinctions. Like the black color he wears and the darkness with which he is obsessed, he creates a realm in which one
cannot tell *this* from *that*. In his incestuous role-playing with
Dorothy, he annihilates the differences among father, husband,
and son. As the kidnapper of her husband and son, he repulses
Dorothy; as her sadist lover, he attracts her. He plays a violent
adult but also a vulnerable child. He wants total control over
Dorothy's behavior, yet he gives over the control of his mind to
nitrous oxide.

Frank, the figure of pure chaos on the surface, seems to be the
polar opposite to the bright world of Jeffrey's father and the lawful
realm of Detective Williams. However, a closer look shows that
Frank is in fact very similar to both men.[25] Like both men, he
reduces difference to the same. If Mr. Beaumont and Detective
Williams can see only luminous order, Frank can perceive only
gloomy chaos. Where Beaumont and Williams reduce the world
to lawful brightness and ignore the unlawful darkness, Frank does
the reverse: he flattens his environment to turbulent anarchy and
represses the possibility of good order. Like Beaumont and
Williams, Frank is a dictator of experience, a rigid presence, fixed
in darkness like a machine in its circuit. For all of his seeming
spontaneity, he is actually as predictable as the night that follows
the day. In spite of his apparent antinomianism, he is really lawful
like a cop.

Indeed, Frank shares several secret affinities with Beaumont and Williams. He is, like Mr. Beaumont, a patriarch. He requires Dorothy to call him "sir" and he refers to himself as "daddy." While Jeffrey's father languishes in the hospital, Frank becomes a surrogate parent for the boy. When he should be visiting his father at the hospital, Jeffrey follows and observes Frank. While at Dorothy's apartment for an assignation, Jeffrey models his actions on Frank's sadistic behavior. Frank resembles Detective Williams in having close connections to the law. His sexuality is extremely rule oriented; he cannot enjoy sex with Dorothy unless she follows his every dictate perfectly. Moreover, he engages in drug deals with a corrupt policeman named Gordon; he even owns a police radio. Finally, he develops a second persona Jeffrey calls the "well-dressed man," a character who wears well-appointed clothes when he works with Gordon.

In light of these affinities, we can conclude that Frank shares the limitations of Mr. Beaumont and Detective Williams. He is unable to enjoy immediate experience. He is fixated on narrow abstractions. Though he seems to be alive, he is really dead. Indeed, Frank, like his two familiars, does not suffer history at all. He seems to have a prefabricated script for most all of his actions, and this script removes contingency from his existence. When he engages in sex with Dorothy, he requires that he and she both fall into predictable roles with specific props and lines. When he behaves violently, he needs Roy Orbison's "In Dreams" to be blaring in the background. When he delivers his lines in public, he requires that his three henchmen laugh at his every sentence. These scripted gestures are not very different from Mr. Beaumont's clichéd suburban lawn watering and Detective Williams's staid police lingo. In all cases, time is made static, dead.

Just as he broke from the behaviors of his father and the laws of Williams, so Jeffrey must separate himself from Frank. He finds, however, that divorcing himself from Frank is not so easy. First of all, he shares with Frank a propensity to break the law; breaking and entering is not far from assault and kidnapping. Second, he actually becomes obsessed with Frank, not only mimicking Frank in bed with Dorothy but also spending his days following the man. Indeed, for a brief time, Jeffrey becomes

Frank. If he is to renounce this stultifying presence, he must kill a part of himself. He can only achieve this self-purgation through the aid of the virginal presence.

Opening to the Other

After his first encounter with Frank, Jeffrey becomes for a time totally preoccupied with him. As we know, stoked by his curiosity over the ear, Jeffrey secretly shadows Frank wherever he goes. Likewise, as we also know, Jeffrey imitates Frank in his brutal lovemaking to Dorothy. But Jeffrey's mirroring of Frank becomes the most intensely intimate during a wild night in which Frank abducts the young man and Dorothy. After discovering Jeffrey leaving Dorothy's apartment and suspecting him of being Dorothy's lover, Frank, with the help of his thugs, forces the two into his car for a "joy ride." In the course of the night—part of which is spent at the bizarre home of Ben (Dean Stockwell), who wears a tuxedo and makeup while lip-synching Roy Orbison's "In Dreams"—Frank concludes that Jeffrey is involved with Dorothy. He takes the boy to a lonely lumberyard. After sniffing his nitrous oxide, he smears his face with lipstick and then does the same to Jeffrey. With "In Dreams" blaring on his car stereo, he beats his double with the same intensity with which he earlier raped Dorothy.[26] Frank incorporates Jeffrey into his dark world. He marks Jeffrey with lipstick that has been on his own mouth, penetrates the boy with his fists, and annihilates the young man's pride. When Jeffrey wakes the next morning in the lumberyard, battered and alone, he is a different person, ostensibly changed forever.

In the next scene, we witness Jeffrey in his room weeping. As a series of images revealing his thoughts shows, he has become fully awakened to Dorothy's terrible plight—she is a mother bereft of her son—and feels terrible remorse for treating her in the same way that Frank was treating her—for violently controlling her actions.[27] Awakened, he further realizes that he must move beyond Frank in the same way that he moved beyond his father's superficial happiness and Detective Williams's rigid laws. He can achieve this transcendence, aptly, only by discovering his own powers of chastity, by becoming like Sandy and Dorothy—by freeing himself from Frank's purely material lusts and finding rebirth in the spirit. In order to achieve this liberation and this discovery, he must purge his materialistic fixations and open himself—as Dorothy and Sandy do—to the ambiguous present, to the flickering mixture of darkness and of light. If he can do this, then he will experience the world's paradoxical beauties—its luminous gloom, its somber gorgeousness. Experiencing this sublime duplicity, he will give himself an opportunity to become a full human being, a capacious creature—not just a half man.

Jeffrey undertakes this quest for vitality by trying to behave toward Sandy and Dorothy in the same way that these women earlier behaved toward him. Part of achieving this goal requires that he rid himself and the world of the influence of Frank. This he attempts by revealing to Detective Williams all of the evidence he has gathered concerning Frank. He clearly hopes that this revelation will purge Frank from his system and cleanse the police department of corruption. After his conversation with Williams, he takes Sandy out to a high school party. There, while they are slow dancing, they kiss each other tenderly and then proclaim their love for one another. Becoming intimate with Sandy, Jeffrey shows himself capable of an emotional sensitivity utterly lacking in Frank, his father, and Williams. In entering into this sweetly amorous relationship with Sandy, Jeffrey indeed relinquishes any desire to control behavior. He becomes vulnerable, risks being hurt. Moreover, he attaches himself to Sandy's soulful idealism, her longing heart. Earlier in the film, after Jeffrey has told her of Frank's criminal acts, Sandy confesses to Jeffrey a dream of cosmic redemption. In this dream, the land is dark and evil, devoid of song and of love. Then, all of the sudden, a huge flock of robins flies in from nowhere. Their music signals affection and light, the return of the land to goodness and joy.

Opening himself to love and hope, Jeffrey mirrors Sandy. He becomes to her what she has been to him: a mixture of light—the possibility of amorous bliss—and darkness—the potential for the wounds of unreturned affection. But Jeffrey also doubles Sandy in another, more complex way. Soon after he vows his love to Sandy, he, along with Sandy, finds a deranged, naked, and beaten Dorothy in his neighborhood. She has been driven mad with grief and terror and seeks aid from Jeffrey. While Jeffrey and Sandy are finding clothing for her and arranging an ambulance, Dorothy in her madness makes it clear that she and Jeffrey were lovers. This prompts Jeffrey soon after to confess to Sandy that he has indeed been Dorothy's lover. He asks her forgiveness. In this act, he in two ways doubles Sandy's qualities. First of all, in admitting his error, he shows that he's not fixated on only one identity. He is capable of shedding an old self in favor of a new one. He becomes vulnerable, open, and flexible. Secondly, in revealing depths under his surface, he embodies an integral relationship between darkness and light. He acknowledges that a sable heart lurks behind the sheen of shining armor. He darkens his luminous exterior and sheds light on his gloomy core. In forgiving Jeffrey his transgression, Sandy acknowledges his duplicitous existence. Her embrace of his imbrications of darkness and light prepares the way for her impending "marriage" with him, a complementary union between a male now able to discover order rising from chaos and a female who understands that chaos underlies all orders.

Jeffrey doubles Dorothy as well. Immediately after finding her wandering naked and insane through his neighborhood, Jeffrey offers her exactly what she needs. He covers her bruised and nude body. He offers her comforting hugs. He calls an ambulance for her. He rides with her to the hospital. He stays with her there until he is sure that she'll be okay. In performing these deeds, Jeffrey guides Dorothy as she earlier guided him. Before this horrific night, Dorothy led Jeffrey from his safe, youthful identity to a more complex manhood. She helped him shed a harmfully stultifying self and embrace a form of being more open to ambiguity, to mystery. Now Jeffrey takes Dorothy from her self-destructive extremes to a more moderate identity. He aids her transformation: from a sadomasochistic sensualist with hope in her heart to a loving mother with a tragic sensibility.

But Jeffrey mirrors Dorothy in a deeper way as well. Right after making sure that she's okay and calling Sandy to confess his affair with Dorothy, Jeffrey decides to return to Dorothy's apartment in hopes of saving her husband and her son. He doesn't need to do this, for the police have already been notified of Frank's criminal actions and are ostensibly in the process of bringing him to justice. But he enters willingly into this dangerous situation anyway. He is obviously keen on experiencing life's mysteries in their most intense, most dangerous forms, even to the point of risking his life. Self-consciously opening himself to life's strangest moments, Jeffrey mimics Dorothy in two fundamental ways. First, in facing Frank alone, he literally puts himself in Dorothy's place. He thus enters into an empathetic relationship with her. He opens his heart to the fear and resilience of another person. Second, in risking his own life, he copies Dorothy's own intimacy with the possibility of death. He thus necessarily imagines his own ego being vanquished and therefore inevitably faces the mystery of losing a stable identity. Undergoing these two modes of transcendence, Jeffrey defeats Frank and helps to recuperate Dorothy. He rids her world of the dictatorial Frank and restores her to her son. Purged of oppression and inspired by love, she will now be able to recover a balance between erotic playfulness and maternal responsibility.

Purging Frank

In battling Frank by himself, Jeffrey puts himself in a position to cleanse himself once and for all of his propensity for emotional tyranny. If he can remove Frank from circulation, he will be able likewise to purge Frank's qualities from his system. In his final showdown with Frank, more than his body is at stake. His very soul is on the line.

When Jeffrey reaches Dorothy's place, he finds two dead men, both shot in the head: a man with only one ear, ostensibly Don, and another in a yellow suit, the corrupt cop. He is saddened by this scene, and actually begins to falter in his quest for self-understanding. He tells himself that the police can handle the situation, and he prepares to leave the apartment. However, just as he passes through Dorothy's door and starts to head down the stairs, he hears Frank in the stairwell below. Jeffrey then sees him: he is disguised as a well-dressed businessman and carrying a police walkie-talkie. Jeffrey takes the police radio from the dead cop and puts it in Dorothy's bedroom. He hides in the closet. Frank enters the apartment. He hears the radio and suspects that Jeffrey is hiding in the bedroom. He fires several bullets into the room. While he is doing this, Jeffrey rushes from the closet, grabs the gun of the dead cop, and returns. When Frank discovers that Jeffrey is not in the room, he eventually makes his way to all the rooms until he settles on the closet. He opens the closet door. Jeffrey shoots him the forehead. Sandy and her father rush in. Detective Williams reassures Jeffrey that it's all over. Sandy and Jeffrey kiss outside of Dorothy's apartment as the bodies are being rolled out.

It appears that Jeffrey has cleverly and with maturity defeated the most unseemly part of himself and, in doing so, he has found a way to merge with Sandy and to liberate Dorothy. The film, it seems, should end here. Jeffrey has completed his quest. Through the aid of Sandy and Dorothy, he has undergone experiences far beyond those of his father, Detective Williams, and Frank. Though these encounters have troubled him deeply, he found ways to transform them into profound knowledge. He now understands that darkness and light, chaos and order, form and formlessness, are mutually inclusive oppositions, with each pole enlivening the other. This realization results in the virginal disposition suggested by the presences of Sandy and Dorothy: the ability to dwell in the physical world without becoming fixated on material forms, to be in the flow and above it.[28]

A New Order

However, the film does not stop here. A denouement follows. This final coda appears to picture Jeffrey reaping the benefits of his hard-earned knowledge—enjoying the light growing from the darkness, reveling in his virginal union with Sandy. All evil has been transmuted into vital energy, all messy matter to pristine spirit.

The film moves from the dark and deadly night in front of Dorothy's building to a brightly lighted ear. In the background is the same syrupy, churchlike tune that accompanied Sandy's earlier revelation of a dream of robins spreading love over the evil land. To the tune, a woman sings these words: "Sometimes a wind blows / and you and I / float / in love / and kiss forever / in a darkness / and the mysteries / of love/ come clear/ and dance / in light / in you / in me / and show / that we / are Love." The camera moves slowly in on the ear and then out again to reveal that the ear is Jeffrey's. He has emerged, so it seems, from the portal of darkness. He is unscathed, yet sadder and wiser. He is lounging in his well-manicured backyard in the bright sun. He is stirred by Sandy calling him for lunch. As he goes in, he greets his healed father and Detective Williams standing in the corner of his lawn and engaged in pleasant conversation. Walking through his house to his kitchen, Jeffrey sees his mother and Mrs. Williams chatting in the living room. In the kitchen, he joins Sandy and his aunt gazing at a robin perched on the windowsill. The bird, which looks to be artificial, holds a writhing beetle in its mouth. Responding to Sandy's fascination over this spectacle, Jeffrey looks at her and says, "Maybe the robins are here." He means the robins of Sandy's dream. The aunt, however, is disgusted by the bird's eating of the beetle. Sandy and Jeffrey smile complacently before Sandy smarmily asks Jeffrey's earlier question, no longer unsettling but cute: "A strange world, isn't it?" Jeffrey smiles knowingly. The camera then returns to the images that opened the film: the tulips and roses blowing before the fence, the fire truck rolling by with a fireman waving and smiling.

One could easily read this sequence as a fitting coda to the film. Jeffrey has now taken the place of his father and is in the process of inaugurating a new family order, one that is sensitive to nuance and ambiguity, polarity and irony. This fresh and welcome pattern is aptly marked by the robin and the beetle, a mixture of artifice and nature, sky and earth, height and depth.[29] Gazing lovingly at this spectacle, Jeffrey and Sandy fully realize what they have achieved: a rare synthesis of matter and spirit, a gnosis of the enduring form organizing the cruel world into a song of love.

The very last scene of the film appears to support this reading. The camera cuts from Jeffrey and Sandy to a park. In this park, a small boy runs in slow motion. The sentimental song about the mystery of love continues to play in the background. The child is wearing the same conical party hat that Jeffrey earlier found in Dorothy's house. The camera moves outward to reveal the goal of the boy's sprint—his mother, Dorothy Vallens. She sits on a park bench wearing an ordinary brown blouse, no longer garbed in velvet robes. Donnie leaps into her arms, and she hugs him happily. However, as she is hugging him, the expression on her face changes to wistful sadness. Her melancholy gaze is matched by an abrupt alteration in the soundtrack. The sugary "Mystery of Love" gives way to the final lines of "Blue Velvet," rendered in Dorothy's heartbreaking voice: "And I still can see blue velvet / Through my tears." During this transition in music, the camera moves away from Dorothy and Donnie and up into the blue sky. This shot fades into the image that opened the movie: a blue velvet curtain shimmering and waving. This final sequence points to this idea: only through embracing the hard, sad reality of loss—lost love and lost loved ones—can one ascend to the boundless sky. Gathering depth and height, one grasps the mystery of polarity, figured by the breathing velvet.

The Return of the Law

However, though these final sequences can be interpreted as instances of the virginal vision, they can also be parsed in another way: as recapitulations of the film's opening panorama and thus as signs that Jeffrey might not have gained transforming knowledge at all.[30] Jeffrey sits in his well-kept lawn with his father and Detective Williams nearby. He does not question their vapid presence in his space. Instead, he has become one with his father's clichéd behavior and Williams's rigid lawfulness. He walks into his house and witnesses the robin holding the beetle. He does not acknowledge this sight as a symbol of synthesis, of the coincidence between idyll and nightmare, beauty and violence. On the contrary, he simply reacts as if he beholds a cute spectacle, an object worthy only of a condescending smile. On both counts—his lounging in the backyard and his watching of the bird—it appears that Jeffrey has settled for empty hierarchy, for Hollywood pastoral exclusive of the soul's wilderness, for static harmony over vital turbulence.

In the penultimate scene, the camera returns to the overly vivid tulips and the fireman waving in slow motion. This repetition of the opening precisely suggests that Jeffrey has not learned anything at all from his deep experiences. He has simply returned to the status quo firmly in place at the film's beginning. In recoiling from the insights gained in the course of his story and fleeing back to the flatland, Jeffrey appears to succumb to a primary temptation of the tepid seeker. For the weak seeker, the conformist on a lark, the darkness, while at first exciting, manifests itself as consuming evil. Encountering this horror, this conformist runs scared, returns to the conventions that earlier ruled his life. Only now he holds the conventions with more intensity than before. He fixates on rules as if they are the only safeguards against the darkness.

The scenes just discussed suggest that Jeffrey learns nothing from his mysterious encounters; the powers of chastity, it appears, are lost on his vacant soul. The final scene intimates Dorothy's similar failure: she is, it seems, unable to benefit from her virginal potency, her ability to move between the darkness and the light. Even though she is reunited with her child, she nonetheless looks wistfully sad, as if she is somehow dissatisfied with motherhood. The soundtrack's return to her melancholy crooning of "Blue Velvet" supports this idea: she is ill-at-ease in her current role as a conventional mother and longs for her past experiences, tragic and painful though they were. While Jeffrey's final comfort encourages him to forget his deep encounters, Dorothy's ultimate well-being makes her wish for the tragic events of her past.

As in *Eraserhead*, Lynch in *Blue Velvet* supports content with form. He appears to be aware of this idea: for a film to be virginal, it must not fixate on any one meaning but must instead prove irreducibly ambiguous. In featuring a hopelessly contradictory ending, Lynch sets his film at odds with itself, erases one theme with another. This self-consummation on one level undercuts the power of virginity, suggests that the vision of chastity is weak, ineffective. But on another level, this very annihilation of the virginal potency proves the ultimate force of chastity by establishing the inexhaustible energy of a form that is formless, an artifact undone by wildness. *Blue Velvet* is endlessly playful, an eternal dance between oppositions—not only between darkness and light but also between cinematic idyll and film noir, spiritual height and material depth, comforting pattern and agitating turbulence.

Vacillating between these and other extremes, the movie is something and nothing at once, both a statement about virginity and a removal of all statements. Promiscuous, it is pure. Untouched, it gives to everyone.

NOTES

1. Chris Rodley, *Lynch on Lynch*, rev. ed. (New York: Faber & Faber, 2005), 139.

2. As Kenneth Kaleta has said, "Lynch's world is not good *or* bad but rather good *and* bad" (*David Lynch* [New York: Twayne, 1993], 97).

3. Martha P. Nochimson indeed claims that the film is ultimately about how certain overly rationalistic forces—like those supported by Detective Williams and Frank Booth—endanger "our connection to the real" and also about how certain more flexible behaviors—like those of Jeffrey—might lead to a version of "manhood more expansive than that of the police or criminals" (*The Passion of David Lynch: Wild at Heart in Hollywood* [Austin: University of Texas Press, 1997], 101).

4. Hans Peter Duerr, *Dreamtime: Concerning the Boundary between Wilderness and Civilization* (Oxford: Blackwell, 1987), 16.

5. Nochimson has said that Jeffrey is indeed Lynch's "first completely developed Hollywood seeker-hero" who quests after a secret held by a feminine power (*Passion of David Lynch*, 99).

6. John Alexander has illuminated one half of this picture, arguing that Jeffrey is on a quest for Dorothy, a form of Aphrodite (*The Films of David Lynch* [London: Charles Letts, 1993], 92). In making this claim, Alexander suggests that Jeffrey is after a certain kind of female power. Duerr would say that this is the power of the *parthenos*, the power that is virginal because it is attached to no one man.

7. Betsy Berry succinctly sums up the duplicity of both women: "Vallens . . . is an ironic mixture of both dark seductress and the woman in peril whom the hero must rescue. Sandy Williams . . . is the opposite end of the scale from Vallens, as the wholesome love interest for the hero; yet she is also a dangerous temptress, stirring Jeffrey into action which can only place him in jeopardy" ("Forever, In My Dreams: Generic Conventions and the Subversive Imagination in *Blue Velvet*," *Literature/Film Quarterly* 16, no. 2 [1988]: 83).

8. Duerr, *Dreamtime*, 16.

9. Bentley Layton, *The Gnostic Scriptures: Ancient Wisdom for the New Age* [New York: Doubleday, 1987], 29–38.

10. Kurt Rudolph, *Gnosis: The Nature and History of Gnosticism*, rev. ed. (San Francisco: HarperSanFrancisco, 1987), 80–83.

11. Jacques Lacarriere, *The Gnostics* (San Francisco: City Lights Press, 1989), 45–50; Rudolph, *Gnosis,* 294–98.

12. Lacarriere, *Gnostics,* 51; Rudolph, *Gnosis,* 297–98.

13. Michel Chion notes that Lynch once said that velvet is "almost organic" (*David Lynch* [London: British Film Institute, 1995], 89). Berry agrees, claiming that this opening blue velvet moves "as if it were a human organ" ("Forever, In My Dreams," 83, 87).

14. Howard Hampton provocatively notes that the "supersaturated colors" of the film point to the false "radiance" of the "Reaganite myth," the artificial colors hiding true violence ("David Lynch's Secret History of the United States," *Film Comment* 29, no. 3 [1993]: 39).

15. Kaleta notes that the owner of the ear, Don Vallens, is likened by Frank to Van Gogh. This connects the ear with artistic development. Jeffrey's embrace of the ear "implies [his] invention and artistic creation within the film" (*David Lynch,* 95). Chion is even more explicit about the ear as a portal between two worlds—the world of stasis and the world of life: "The ear functions as a passageway, the symbol of communication between two worlds. The ear transmits the gift of passing through the surface, of traveling between worlds, then recovering a normal world. Frank thus offers Jeffrey a key to life and a gift of the imagination. In short, everything in *Blue Velvet* has a dynamic sense of life" (*David Lynch,* 97).

16. Many have written on this film as a depiction of Jeffrey's development. For instance, Lynne Layton in her Freudian reading argues that it is a "parable of male development, a parable in which one grows from power as a male baby, rid of the father and in possession of the mother, to impotence as a man" ("*Blue Velvet*: A Parable of Male Development," *Screen* 35, no. 4 [1994]: 381). Janet Preston claims that the film depicts an "initiation journey" into hell, where Jeffrey discovers dark depths about himself that his sterile, middle-class environment could never offer ("Dantean Imagery in *Blue Velvet,*" *Literature/ Film Quarterly* 18, no. 3 [1990]: 167). Michael Moon claims that Jeffrey undergoes two simultaneous initiations based on the film's two interwoven plots. In one plot, Jeffrey "must negotiate what is represented as being the treacherous path between an older, ostensibly exotic, sexually 'perverse' woman and a younger, racially 'whiter,' sexually 'normal' one, and he must at the same time and as part of the same process negotiate an even more perilous series of interactions with the older woman's violent and murderous criminal lover and the younger woman's protective police-detective father. This heterosexual plot resolves itself in classic Oedipal fashion: the young man, Jeffrey, destroys the demonic criminal 'father' and rival, Frank; rescues the older woman, Dorothy, from Frank's sadistic clutches; and then relinquishes her to her fate and marries the perky young daughter of the good cop" ("A Small Boy and Others: Sexual Disorientation in Henry James, Kenneth Ager, and David Lynch," in *Comparative American Identities: Race, Sex, and Nationality in the Modern Text,* ed. Hortense J. Spillers,

141–56 [New York: Routledge, 1991], 144). But there is a second developmental plot, in which Jeffrey is initiated into a "perverse" world in which "characters enact a whole series of uncanny relationships between males of different ages, social classes, and supposed sexual orientations—orientations which get thoroughly disoriented when they get swept near the flame of 'perverse' desire that flows around the figures of the chief sadomasochistic pair, Frank and Dorothy" (ibid., 145). In both cases, Jeffrey must move through an ordeal that calls his very identity into question.

17. Many have noted the rather obvious "noir" elements of the film: the morally ambiguous detective, the dark lady, the violent criminal, the good girl, the seedy crime underbelly, etc. Indeed, as Fred Pfeil has noted, it "is too easy to tick off the *noir* elements" in the film." "Any sophomore," he continues, "with an introductory film course can pick out these features" ("Home Fires Burning: Family *Noir* in *Blue Velvet* and *Terminator 2*," in *Shades of Noir*, ed. Joan Copjec, 227–60 [New York: Verso, 1993], 231). Just as "anyone," he goes on, "with an introductory psychology course can pick up on the Oedipal motifs hiding in plain sight." Pfeil goes on to show how the film purveys a vision of "family noir," based on the idea that any family in mimicking cultural clichés is actually inhabited and haunted by an "other" and in the end is little different than a machine (ibid., 231–38). Judith Bryant Wittenberg and Robert Gooding-Williams argue that the film employs noir images of women in order simultaneously to objectify women and to subvert these very objectifications ("The 'Strange World' of *Blue Velvet*: Conventions, Subversions, and Representations of Women," in *Sexual Politics and Popular Culture*, ed. Diane Raymond, 149–57 [Bowling Green: Bowling Green State University Popular Press, 1990]).

18. Paul Coughlin believes that the film endlessly parodies these and other cultural conventions. In doing so, the movie helps viewers understand the idea that these conventions are oppressive constructs that can be challenged and ultimately transcended ("*Blue Velvet*: Postmodern Parody and the Subversion of Conservative Frameworks," *Literature/Film Quarterly* 31, no. 4 [2003]: 304–5).

19. Wittenberg and Gooding-Williams show how Lynch "complicates our reactions" to the "female archetypes" of Dorothy and Sandy by "departing from the norm." While Dorothy is the classic femme fatale of the noir world, she is also a victim of evil. Likewise, even though Sandy is the typical innocent of film noir, she also shows qualities of the femme fatale ("The 'Strange World' of *Blue* Velvet," 155). Chion argues that the two women are mirror images of one another in such a way that they seem to compose "two sides of one figure, each side endlessly leading to the other as in a Möbius strip" (*David Lynch*, 91).

20. Very few readers have seen beyond the shallow idea that the film is misogynistic and realized that the women in the movie are vital, complex figures. As noted, Alexander (*Films of David Lynch*) sees Dorothy as an

"Aphrodite" figure, a goddess with transforming potency. Also as noted, Wittenberg and Gooding-Williams ("The 'Strange World' of *Blue* Velvet") argue that Sandy and Dorothy alike are complex, duplicitous characters. Another reading positive toward women—in this case toward Sandy—is Tracy Biga's. Biga argues that the movie "offers a case study in how women watch men and how the relation of a person looking and a person looked at may depict formulations other than control and power" ("Review of *Blue Velvet*," *Film Quarterly* 41, no. 1 [Autumn 1987]: 44). A part of this argument is this: Sandy's view of the world is a powerful lens through which audiences understand that the apparent simplicity of the film's ending hides "mystery" (ibid., 48, 49). I should here note, too, that Norman K. Denzin believes that the film, while sexist in its depiction of Sandy as the pure, innocent girl, parodies and undercuts the "'playboy' woman of soft pornography" by photographing Dorothy in a hyperrealist fashion in her nude scenes (*Images of Postmodern Society: Social Theory and Contemporary Cinema* [London: Sage, 1991], 76).

21. Here it is appropriate to note what Isabella Rossellini herself had to say about Lynch's religious thrust in the film: "A lot of people thought it [the film] was sick, but for me it always represented the research in David of the good and the bad. He's quite a religious person. Quite spiritual. Any person who is religious is always trying to define these things, which are so elusive. I think that's the core of his film-making" (Quoted in Chris Rodley, *Lynch on Lynch*, rev. ed. [New York: Faber & Faber, 2005], 126).

22. Michel Chion in *David Lynch* makes the comparison of the film to this seventies sit-com (83).

23. In *Secret Cinema*, I argue that Jeffrey's quest is alchemical. My current reading is in some ways a version of that one, though here I put less emphasis on the importance of Frank in Jeffrey's development.

24. Some representative Freudian readings are Barbara Creed, "A Journey through *Blue Velvet*: Film, Fantasy, and the Female Spectator," *New Formations* 7 (1988): 95–115; Laura Mulvey, "The Pre-Oedipal Father: The Gothicism and *Blue Velvet*," in *Modern Gothic: A Reader*, ed. Victor Sage and Allan Lloyd Smith, 38–57 (New York: Manchester University Press, 1996); James Lindroth, "Down the Yellow Brick Road: Two Dorothys and the Journey of Initiation in Dream and Nightmare," *Literature/Film Quarterly* 18, no. 3 (1990): 160–66; Lynne Layton and Sam Ishii-Gonzales, "Mysteries of Love: Lynch's *Blue Velvet*/Freud's Wolf-Man," in *The Cinema of David Lynch: American Dreams, Nightmare Visions*, ed. Erica Sheen and Annette Davison, 48–60 (New York: Wallflower Press, 2005).

25. In this section I closely follow Nochimson, who argues that "Frank and Detective Williams [are] two parts of the same self-referential rational culture." Jeffrey must go beyond the "borders" embodied by both of these characters, she continues, "into vision" (*Passion of David Lynch*, 101).

26. Many have noted the homoerotic relationship between Frank and Jeffrey. The representative reading in this line is Michael Moon's.

27. Nochimson influences me here, yet again. She argues that Jeffrey, after Frank beats him, cries tears of "remorse" for Dorothy's "suffering and self-loathing" (*Passion of David Lynch*, 117).

28. This is a perfect example of what Nochimson calls Jeffrey's "receptive masculinity" (*Passion of David Lynch*, 113). Reaching this state, Jeffrey moves beyond a desire to "control and masculine aggression" (ibid., 103).

29. Nochimson maintains that the robin is indeed a satisfying ending, for the bird embodies Lynch's favorite "mystical truth": "as above, so below" (*Passion of David Lynch*, 122). She comments further that this bird marks a place where "culture and energy are briefly revealed in balance. Robin and insect at this moment constitute and make visible a Lynchian, asymmetrical balance of human and eternal forces. This is also Lynch's homage to Jeffrey's achievement in accessing a larger order" (ibid.). I of course believe that the bird is satisfying and unsatisfying at once.

30. Wittenberg and Gooding-Williams mark the irreducible duplicity of Lynch's film: "Lynch's ludic and stylish film . . . makes it difficult to formulate perspectives. We cannot comfortably navigate its strange world" ("The 'Strange World' of *Blue* Velvet," 157).

CHAPTER THREE

Sacred Sensuality in *Wild at Heart*

Love among the Ruins

Soon after making *Wild at Heart*, a film loosely based on Barry Gifford's novel of the same name, a reporter asked Lynch what inspired him about the story. Lynch's answer was immediate and clear. He was most drawn, he said, to the intense romance between Sailor Ripley (Nicholas Cage) and Lula Fortune (Laura Dern). He found these characters, he continued, to be perfectly compatible. Sailor exhibited extremely masculine traits, but he felt a deep respect for Lula's strong femininity; Lula demonstrated very feminine characteristics yet showed a profound regard for Sailor's robust manliness. This complementarity—Sailor's sensitive masculinity coupled with Lula's virile femininity—allowed these characters, in Lynch's mind, to find comfort in a "strange world," to stand side by side in the face of terrible adversity. Finding affection in the waste, Sailor and Lula constituted, Lynch concluded, "a really modern romance in a violent world," a way of "finding love in hell."[1]

Embedded in these remarks is a theory of love, of *amor*.[2] Lynch suggests that what moved him most about the story was not merely its erotic force or its unsettling world. What inspired him most was the combination between the two: the idea that love most fully burns in the midst of wreckage, that the wasteland is the muse of romance. This notion suggests that a certain kind of romantic love grows out of and transcends all that is not love. This sort of *amor*, regardless of its erotic intensity, can only be called spiritual, religious, for it is redemptive, an elevation of bliss out of ruin. Indeed, a major part of this kind of love *is* its erotic intensity: the more earnest the contact between bodies, the more powerful the lift to transcendence. This situation is of course paradoxical on two levels: earthly destruction encourages amorous joy; physical intimacy generates spiritual redemption. What vision is capacious enough to contain these contradictions?

In medieval Provence, numerous troubadours traveled from court to court singing of a certain kind of love. These itinerant minstrels were deeply influenced by Gnostic and Sufi ideas of *amor*. These ideas were based on the notion that passionate love between the sexes is the proper mystical mode. Only through impassioned love toward a particular individual can a man or a woman achieve union with the divine. In this view, marriage is beside the point: only the passion of love is important, and this passion is generally all the stronger when it takes place outside of wedlock. Embracing this dangerous theory, most troubadours of medieval Provence faced fatal persecution from a Catholic Church bent on upholding the sacrament of marriage. For many of these wandering singers of love, *amor* was literally the reverse of *Roma*: impassioned, extramarital love with an individual ran counter to the stilted marital rules of the Holy See. Impassioned love grew out of a rebellion against a destructive church, and this sort of heretical *amor* persisted in the face of possible death at the hands of the Inquisition. Emerging from a violently oppressive landscape, this kind of love offered an escape from the tyranny of institutional evil, an intimate respite, however brief, from the world's pernicious divisions. In the love embrace, one could become, for a time, human.

In inflecting this idea of love, *Wild at Heart* obviously shares with *Eraserhead* and *Blue Velvet* this emphasis: immediate experience is superior to abstract authority. Each of these films challenges the concepts that circumscribe behavior and encourages openness toward the mysterious particular. *Eraserhead* champions sacred silence over the boisterous divisions of language. *Blue Vel-*

vet lauds flexible ambiguity over clichés and laws. In the same way, *Wild at Heart* extols unmediated amorous contact over the stultifying conventions of marriage; it praises, as it were, *amor* over *Roma*. In *Wild at Heart*, Sailor and Lula seek Gnostic liberation from the abstractions that ignore love. This rebellion resembles the "left-hand path" of certain Gnostic sects, the commitment to antinomian action, to the exhaustion of sensual passion. But this unsettling Gnostic current is not mere libertinism, not simple hedonism. On the contrary, this erotic Gnosticism also requires a strict discipline that recalls "right-hand" modes as well. To achieve this sort of sensual Gnostic liberation, one must achieve bodily grace, an elegant attunement to the beautiful mysteries of the flesh. Between dark contrarianism and bright asceticism, this Gnostic eroticism is simultaneously turbulent and cultivated, wild at heart yet courtly in demeanor.

Sailor and Lula aspire to this balance between burning desire and noble carriage.[3] Entrapped in a landscape of pervasive wickedness—an environment beset by tyranny and violence, deceit and death—Sailor and Lula can only look to their love for salvation. From the surrounding darkness, there blooms in these young characters an exquisite passion. This erotic energy allows them to escape for a time the painful evil of their world. Still, even though they are consumed by a fiery lust, they nonetheless exhibit a sweet sensitivity to one another's needs, a graceful attunement to the longings of the heart. This elegant attention is gorgeous in form, a mannered dance.

As was the case with *Eraserhead* and *Blue Velvet*, Lynch in *Wild at Heart* supports his content with his form. His film is a bizarre mixture of reassuring cinematic conventions and disturbing scenes of violence. One minute, the film features Sailor breaking into an Elvis-inspired rendition of "Love Me" at a dance club. The next minute, the movie shows a woman horrifically dying in the aftermath of a car wreck. One minute, the picture depicts Lula envisioning characters from *The Wizard of Oz*. The next, the film renders Lula undergoing a sinister rape at the hands of a hardened criminal. This clash of moods makes the film analogous to the amorous relationship between Sailor and Lula, a blend of brutal eroticism and tender affection. The question concerning both the forms, the cinematic and the amorous, is this: is synthesis achieved, a concord of opposites, or is fracture perpetrated, a severing of potential affinities?

In Lynch's problematic picture, the answer to both of these questions is actually yes. The film's key theme—the amorous link between fire and ice—and the film's primary form—cinematic coincidence of evil and sweetness—finds in the end tranquility. Hence, we can rest assured that strange antagonisms will one day cohere, that love indeed can conquer all. But the movie's primary motifs also ultimately dissolve into fragments. Therefore, we are left wondering where the hope lies, where we can ever find concordant bliss in a world of evil tyranny. The movie at the close of the day cancels itself out, and leaves us hovering in an interpretive limbo from which it seems impossible to leave.

We wonder about the nature of this self-consummation: does it undercut the efficacy of amorous love, or does it somehow offer a strong support to this same sort of affection? This erasure obviously achieves both at once, both an annihilation of love and an enhancement of affection. But in embodying these opposing positions at the same time, the film actually supports Gnostic eroticism in a deeper way, a way that goes beyond mere doctrinal support. In transcending dualism, the movie proves thoroughly antinomian, an affront to the pervasive hierarchies of mainstream society. Challenging traditional relationships between the wild body and the disciplined soul, the film moreover points to a synthetic third term beyond opposition, a *tertium quid* that heals all wounds. What would this third position be but a playful *amor* reconciling passion and gentleness? What would it be but an impossible love amidst the ruins?

The Sacred *Amor* of the Troubadours

Wandering around southern France between 1100 and 1300, amorous troubadours such as Peire Vidal, Bertram de Born, and Guiraut de Bornelh entertained numerous moods of love. Still, regardless of their different attitudes, these and other troubadours shared two overarching ideas: the Church of Rome is an evil oppressor of romantic love; liberation from this tyranny requires unbridled amorous passion. Embracing these ideas, the troubadours provide a powerful context for interpreting the redemptive passions of Lynch's *Wild at Heart*.

Scholars have tended to interpret the amorous works of the troubadours in one of three ways. Some scholars have lauded the troubadours for being the first artists in the West to celebrate chaste love. Other scholars have found this reading to be limited, for it overlooks the blatantly erotic qualities of the songs. Yet a third camp takes a middle way between these two divergent schools of thought. Scholars espousing this third position believe the troubadours' erotic intensity was tantamount to spiritual purity.[4]

This third conception of the troubadours is based on the theory that these poets were profoundly influenced by a heresy running rampant in medieval Provence. This heresy was Gnostic, and it was known as Catharism. During the years of the Byzantine Empire, many strains of Manichean Gnosticism persisted. This dualistic worldview made its way to Bulgaria, where it flourished in the tenth century under the name of Bogomilism. For these latter-day Gnostics, spirit—emanating as it did from a perfect God of light—was good, while matter—issuing as it did from Satan, a darkly corrupt son of God—was horror. From this dualistic view came the idea that the physical world was the product of an ignorant maker, Satan himself, and that orthodox priests were unwittingly this demiurge's servants. The only way to endure this polluted plane was to practice a vigorous asceticism, to avoid the generative energies of matter.[5]

The Cathars of the southern regions of France inherited this hope for spiritual purity; indeed, Cathar is the Provençal word for "pure." Like their Bulgarian predecessors, these purists rejected the teachings of the orthodox church and questioned the importance of physical existence. The Cathars were especially dubious of the Catholic sacrament of marriage, for this practice extolled the political powers of the material world and indeed propagated evil procreation. Loathing this world, the Cathars preached chastity and eschewed marriage. These practices freed woman from being seen as mere sex objects and allowed them more prestige than did

Christianity. Thus, these practices, regardless of their roots in asceticism, opened the door for a new notion of sexuality: a sexuality liberated from marital procreation and devoted to equality between woman and man.[6]

This third theory of the troubadours—these wandering minstrels celebrated sex as a sacred act—is grounded on a second notion: these poets were also influenced by Sufism, an Islamic school of mysticism. This mixture of Manichean dualism, Neoplatonism, and Islam came to the southern regions of France by way of Andalusia. This country thrived in the early Middle Ages beside the Spain that for years was under Islamic dominion. During this time, roughly around the tenth and eleventh centuries, Andalusia enjoyed a period of intense lyric poetry. This poetry was affected by Arabic love poetry. The forms and motifs of this Andalusian verse made their way to Languedoc and Poitou.[7]

A major component of this Arabic love poetry was Sufism, a primary school of Islamic mysticism. Though Sufism, like Gnosticism, is a heterogeneous movement, it features a certain recurring theme: the only way to know God is through love. According to the Sufi view, every creature in the cosmos is filled with a longing for its creator. Thus almost all actions are love songs for the eternal beloved. Accordingly, love between a man and a woman is divine love. Behind the male and the female alike is the face of the divine. To pine for this human beloved is to yearn for the God within. To embrace the flesh is to touch God. Such tactile contact with God transforms matter from darkness to light. It reveals the true nature of the world.[8]

This Gnostic current and this Sufi strain suggest that love beyond the constraints of marriage and procreation is the path to the divine. Freed from stifling institutions and the push for generation, this kind of love is free to pursue individuated *amor*. This form of love is keenly experiential. It depends on a concrete, tactile encounter with living and breathing flesh. It requires a tender pressing of *this* person in *this* moment. It necessitates a heart beating for an immanent divinity present in the particular. Merging with this divinity humming in the loins, one cares nothing for dogmas or doctrines. One is passionate only for knowledge, for immediate acquaintance: for gnosis.[9]

Marietta's Will to Power

The wicked world in *Wild at Heart*—it's "wild at heart," Lula says, and "weird on top"—makes it almost impossible for love to exist at all. Indeed, virtually every force in this sinister environment is diametrically opposed to *amor*. The evil genius behind this wasteland of no affection is Marietta Fortune (Diane Ladd), Lula's mother. Like the Gnostic demiurge and the priests unwittingly serving him, Marietta diligently works to control and finally squelch the amorous impulses around her. She does so because she most wants total security. But what she doesn't realize is this: the total security of the police state leads to utter stasis, a world in which difference is reduced to the same. This is the world of death, where nothing changes, nothing strives, nothing loves, nothing *exists*.

The film's analogue for Marietta is the Wicked Witch from the 1939 cinematic version of *The Wizard of Oz*. Like this witch, Marietta opposes the quest to find the ideal home, the place in which one can comfortably love and be loved.[10] Through her various surveillance agents—Johnny Farragut (Harry Dean Stanton), Marcellus Santos (J. E. Freeman), Mr. Reindeer (William Morgan Sheppard), Perdita (Isabella Rossellini), and Bobby Peru (Willem Dafoe)—Marietta enjoys the equivalent of the witch's crystal ball and her flying broomstick. She can basically track every move of Sailor and Lula—the film's collective version of Dorothy. She stalks her daughter and her daughter's lover in hopes of killing Sailor and possessing her daughter. She hates and fears love and longs to destroy it.

The reasons behind Marietta's desire to destroy Lula and Sailor's *amor* are complex. First of all, she appears to confuse love and possession. Before Lula and Sailor even met, she hired Santos to kill her husband by burning him to death and then making the whole affair look like a suicide. This murder suggests that Marietta can only love what she can totally control. When her beloved becomes unruly—an obstacle to her selfish pleasure—she must destroy him. This crusade to slay what she cannot tyrannize reveals her true identity: she is an extreme narcissist, someone who can't discern between self and other. She most desires to impose her will upon her world. When a subject will not bend to her will, she simply removes it, destroys it. For her, love is narcissism, self-love. *Amor*—the selfless passion for another—is for her unthinkable, impossible. Narcissistically confusing affection with possession, Marietta can't stand it when Lula doesn't simply bend to her will. She requires that her daughter serve as an extension of her self. When her girl directs her affection toward Sailor, Marietta sets out to destroy her daughter in the same way that she annihilated her husband. Though Marietta does not want literally to remove her daughter—doesn't wish to murder her—she desires to squelch her daughter's freedom, to reduce her girl to an automaton.[11]

A second reason that Marietta pursues Sailor and Lula is this: Sailor, of all people, is an especial threat to her will to control. This is so for two reasons. First of all, Sailor is in a position to know about Marietta's and Santos's murder of Lula's father. Before Sailor met Lula, he was Santos's driver. Marietta and Santos alike rightly believe that Sailor is aware of their murder, and they thus fear that he will one day reveal their plot. They need to remove him to retain their control over their circumstances. But Marietta also wishes to kill Sailor for a more complex reason: he once rejected her lusty advances toward him. One evening in a Cape Fear dance hall, she attempted to seduce Sailor in the men's toilet. When he turned her away, she immediately threatened to have him killed, and, indeed, minutes later hired Bob Ray Lemon (George Dandridge) to stab Sailor to death. This conflation of lust and violence of course yet again reveals Marietta's narcissism: if she can't have Sailor for her own, no one can have him. But this merging of libido and murder also reveals something even more sinister about Marietta: she wants to steal her own daughter's youth. Jealous of her pretty daughter's ability to garner the love of a handsome man like Sailor, she tries to steal this marker of her girl's youth and thus feel young again herself. When this fails, she takes revenge—not only on Sailor but also on her daughter. She must kill what she fears—the youthful vitality that highlights her old age.

Marietta is against love and life. Both are threats to her desired sovereignty. These spontaneous, flexible, sensitive energies challenge her predictable, fixed, and cruel characteristics. To remain who she is, she must attack these salubrious forces. Her very identity depends on the creation of a wasteland where no love lives.

Love over Tyranny

Sailor and Lula must from the beginning struggle against Marietta's efforts to divide and destroy them. Their romance is constantly threatened by her wicked powers. They must love and live desperately, wildly, if they are ever to achieve safety from Marietta's wicked wiles. They appear to realize this. Almost every time they feel Marietta's oppressive presence, they embrace all the harder. Their *amor* grows out of hell.

Marietta first tries to destroy these two young lovers by hiring Bob Ray Lemon to stab Sailor to death. Sailor violently retaliates. He brutally kills Lemon with his bare hands. For this act, he serves a brief prison sentence for manslaughter. On the day he is released, Lula, against Marietta's commands, picks him up at the Pee Dee Correctional Institute. In the face of Marietta's tyranny, the two quickly recover their intimacy, their concord. Lula brings Sailor's favorite snakeskin jacket. When he asks her if he has ever told her that this jacket is a "symbol" of his "individuality and his belief in personal freedom," she replies gently that he has told her this about a thousand times. This short exchange reminds both characters of their history with one another and also reveals Lula's tender tolerance for Sailor's idiosyncrasies, his strangely individual quirks. (Sailor will return this favor later, when he similarly accepts Lula's propensity for *non sequitor* tales of misery.) Immediately after this exchange, Lula reports that she's reserved a room at the Cape Fear Hotel and planned for both of them to spend an evening dancing at the Hurricane, a club nearby. Sailor anticipates her announcement of the dancing and says the word "Hurricane" at the exact same time as Lula does. This synchronized discourse highlights their harmony with one another, their remarkable attentiveness and responsiveness to each other's thoughts, their willingness to be open to difference.

Sailor and Lula appear to understand that their every act of benevolent tolerance and sensitive responsiveness is a rebellion against the intolerance and insensitivity of Marietta and the oppressive world that she creates. In the very next scene, Sailor and Lula make passionate, mutually satisfying love in their hotel room at the Cape Fear. Soon afterwards, the camera focuses on the ignition of a single wooden match and then on the ignition of a sole cigarette. This is the wild fire of Lula and Sailor's shared passion, a fire that runs counter to the destructive fire with which Marietta murdered her husband.[12] This picture of creative fire is followed by a scene in which Sailor and Lula casually chat in their darkened chamber, a seemingly self-contained and timeless world impervious to outside influences. After Lula praises Sailor for his lovemaking, she recalls how her mother treated her sexuality when she was fifteen years old. Sailor then reminds her that she was raped by one "Uncle Pooch" when she was thirteen. This remark causes Lula to flash back on the scene: she's young and in hair curlers; her mouth is bleeding; an older man who's just raped her disdainfully throws her stockings at her; her mother walks in and begins violently berating the man. Only three months later, she reports, Pooch was killed in a car accident while he was on vacation at Myrtle Beach. Soon after she recounts this story, Lula hears a woman cackling in a nearby room. She tells Sailor that this laughter reminds her of the Wicked Witch from The *Wizard of Oz*. This association is shorthand for her mother's world and all that it entails: violation and murder, loss of innocence and vengeful plots. As if feeling the threat from Marietta, Sailor reassures Lula that the sound simply comes from an "old gal" having a good time. He then reasserts their intimacy by reporting that he's ready to go dancing—to move his body in synchronization with hers, to merge wildness and form.

This is the first of many bedroom sequences in which Lula and Sailor doggedly attempt to keep Marietta's world at bay. In each case, the two lovers confirm their *amor* as the only mode of life amidst the ruins, of salvation in the waste. After Sailor encourages Lula to come dancing with him, the camera cuts to a scene that features Marietta cunningly encouraging Johnny Farragut, her putative lover, to trail Sailor and Lula. After reminding the audience of the sinister environment in which the young lovers move, the film returns to their dimly lighted, self-contained, and seemingly timeless room. There, while Lula's just-painted toenails are drying, Sailor wonders why her mother hounds them. Though he doesn't share this information with Lula, he suspects that she is out to kill him because he rejected her sexual advances and because he knows too much about the death of Lula's father. Instead of dwelling on these dark possibilities, he once more encourages the dance and inspires Lula to hop joyously on their unkempt bed. The cotton between her toes flies wildly in the air.

After the two lovers go dancing at the club (where Sailor defends Lula from a would-be suitor and then sings Elvis's "Love Me"), they return to their room and once more engage in passionate, mutually satisfying sex. After their raucous love-making, we see the postcoital couple lying comfortably in bed, with their heads at opposite ends but their legs intertwined. Lula, as is her wont, alludes to her melancholy life. She asks if Sailor has ever heard in the midst of a wind the laughing of the Wicked Witch. When she makes this inquiry, she flashes back to the other fire in her life, the fire of destruction that killed her father. She then quickly changes the subject and begins talking about smoking—when she started and the brand she chose. The conversation eventually turns to Sailor's own difficult upbringing and his praise of Lula for standing by him even after he served time in prison. After the two lovers sit up to face one another, Lula replies by saying that she'd go to the ends of the earth for Sailor because he "marks her the deepest." She then compares him to her beloved dead father and inquires if he knows how her father died. This question again conjures up the image of the destructive fire, this time for both Sailor and Lula. Sailor begins to confess to Lula that he as Santos's driver was present the night Lula's father was burned to death. Instead, he caresses her exposed left breast and begins to make love to her again. As was the case earlier, the two lovers actively repress their painful lives through their love for one another. With Marietta and her destructive fires burning in the background, Sailor and Lula foster their single creative flame, their tiny light in the middle of lurid annihilation.

The next time Sailor and Lula find themselves together in a bedroom is in New Orleans. Sailor has decided to jump parole and head with Lula out to "sunny California," a region the two liken to Oz, a beautiful destination at the end of the yellow brick road, a place where all wishes come true. As the two are making their way west, they stop in New Orleans for a brief stay. In their hotel room—again dimly lighted and seemingly isolated from the stark and cruel world outside—they once more make wild love. Afterwards, they again lie together in bed, this time side by side. Now on the run from the law and facing the possibility of Sailor's returning to jail, they nonetheless engage in relaxed conversation about their favorite subject: their love for one another. Lula lauds Sailor for being so "responsive" to her during their sex. He pays "attention," she says. She almost feels as though his "sweet cock" has a little voice that talks to her when he's inside of her. She ends by claiming that Sailor really "gets on" her. Sailor, with a satisfied smile on his face, responds by calling Lula "dangerously cute." This mutual acknowledgement of each other's paradoxical virtues flies right in the face of Marietta's narcissism. Lula lauds Sailor for being an aggressive yet sensitive lover, while Sailor praises Lula for being a cuddly but edgy girlfriend. In both cases, the lovers exhibit a feeling for each other's full and complex humanity, an acute, flexible, and lithe sense of the play of existence, its strange interactions between dynamic oppositions.[13]

After going out into the "crazy world" of New Orleans to enjoy a "fried banana sandwich," the two once more retire to their room for their favorite pastime. After their wild sex, they again engage in postcoital colloquy. Lula wonders what it would be like if they could always stay deeply in love. Sailor says from now on, he'll be true only to Lula. He'll never do anything again without a good reason, he claims, and then acknowledges that there are numerous bad ideas out in the world that might tempt a man away from his path. He's obviously thinking of his troubled past, especially of his time with the murderer Santos. Lula responds by telling Sailor a story about bad ideas, a story with a "moral." She then launches into a disturbing tale about her Cousin Dell (Crispin Glover), a mentally ill relative who craved Christmas all year round, feared aliens in black gloves, enjoyed putting cockroaches on his anus, and eventually simply disappeared one day. The unspoken moral of this tale is really the moral of the movie: if one becomes fixated on one idea at the expense of all others, one turns narcissistic, incapable of giving or receiving love, unable to relate at all to the world's sweet particulars. This moral of course also entails the reverse: to remain open, elastic, is to be sensitive to the sacred fluxes and interchanges of *amor*, to the individual beauties of this person, right now.

What empowers this latter capacity is the ability to enjoy ironic interplay. Sailor and Lula in the safety of their love bowers discover middle grounds between form and wildness, pattern and turbulence. Both are wild at heart, keenly enamored of the crazed forces of their fiery passion, of unbridled dancing, of boisterous heavy metal music. But at the same time, both are acutely aware of studied forms—of the courtly sensitivity of their choreographed lovemaking, of the returning rhythm of the dance, of the repetitious beat of head-banging tunes. Undercutting structure with chaos, organizing chaos with structure, both, in their best moments, live beyond oppositions, in those spaces, barely perceivable, where antinomies meet and merge and finally disappear. In these psychic regions, one is untroubled by "hang-ups," by fixations and obsessions, by narcissistic tyranny. One indeed opens one's loving heart to the strange, the unknown—the inexhaustible mystery of the particular. This is the secret of romantic love, of *amor*. Such secrets elude those like Marietta, who fixate on life's extremes—either total control or utter madness. These are Marietta's vacillations. One minute, she desperately tries to police the life of her daughter, to order perfectly her cosmos. The next minute, she falls into insane fits of rage and jealousy, into bouts that border on real insanity. Unable to find the golden mean, the sacred middle of transcendental irony, she ossifies at the extreme, turning life into death, love into hate: the pulsating heart into stone.

The Loss of the Real

But the balance between Sailor and Lula cannot last. From the time that they leave New Orleans until the film's end, they watch their *amor* slowly dissolve. The forces of Marietta and her minions, so it seems, are too much for them. Traveling through a wasteland of death and despair, they soon yield to the pervasive wildness alone and lose their sweet forms of love. They for a time become one with Marietta's hatred.

The last minute we witness Sailor and Lula in perfect harmony
with one another occurs only miles west of New Orleans. They are
making their way toward Texas, where Sailor will try to discover if
Marietta has put a contract on his head. Sailor sleeps in the back-
seat while Lula drives. Lula tries to find pleasing music on the
radio, the kind of rhythm that she and Sailor have enjoyed on their
trip heretofore. All she can tune, however, are stories about sick-
ness, suffering, murder, even cannibalism. She abruptly stops the
car, leaps out, and demands that Sailor find some good music.
Sailor quickly finds a heavy metal station, yells wildly, handsprings
out of the car, and begins to dance in his inimitable fashion—by
punching and kicking to the beat. Lula likewise starts to dance in
her own way, by jumping and stomping like a crazed banshee. The
two then hug each other tenderly, holding desperately onto their
love in the middle of a hot desert. The same somber music that
played over the film's opening credits drowns out the raucous
metal. This music recalls the image accompanying the credits—a
huge and hungry fire, a fire likely destroying all things in its path,
the fire probably that burned Lula's father to death. This same sinister music likewise overruns the voices of Lula and Sailor. They
appear to tell each other that they love one another, but we can't
tell for sure. The camera then pans away from them to take in the
large panorama of natural waste. There they are, the two young
lovers, almost swallowed up by the endless desert and the ravenous
fire. The hell that inspired their love will soon consume them.

In the next scene devoted to these two characters, Sailor and
Lula for the first time drive at night. They make their way down a
dark highway snaking through the middle of the Southwestern
desert. Chris Isaac's sinister instrumental to "Wicked Game" plays
in the background. Sailor reveals to Lula his dark side, his secret
side. He confesses to her that he knew Lula's father and that he sat
outside of her house in Santos's car the night her house burned.
She realizes that he in effect witnessed her father's murder.
Shaken, she tells Sailor that nothing is really as it seems: outward
appearances block access to the real. She then sees flying beside
their car her mother as the Wicked Witch. The Witch cackles. This
is apt, for it is her mother's pervasive presence that now indirectly
causes Lula's discomfort and that harbingers the next catastrophe.

This catastrophe occurs only minutes later, when Sailor and Lula happen upon a terrible car accident off the side of the road. They make their way in the darkness to an overturned car. A passenger lies dead. They then notice a voice. One of the passengers, a teenage girl (Sherilyn Fenn), is alive. She wanders through the dark desert deliriously. She is hallucinating. She talks to people who aren't really present. Soon after, she dies a gruesome death, vomiting blood as she loses consciousness.

This horrible scene is actually a complement to Sailor's earlier confession concerning his past. In both sequences, forms belie realities. Sailor's appearance has hidden his true past. Though he has seemed to be entirely noble, he has in actuality been harboring a terrible secret—he was once one of Marietta's pawns. The dying girl's hallucinations highlight this collapse between form and reality. She believes that she sees a man named Robert, but he in reality is not there. She simply can't tell the difference between what is real and what isn't, between illusion and truth.

These are the collapses of Marietta's world, a world in which one can never tell the difference between appearance and reality. Marietta through her machinations generates an environment in which no one can trust anyone. She deceives Farragut into thinking she's in love with him. She does this only to convince him to go after Sailor and Lula. Later, she deceives Santos in the same way in hopes of persuading him to kill Sailor. This latter action sets in motion an entire sequence of deception. Santos enlists Mr. Reindeer to put a contract out on Sailor. Reindeer hires Sailor's former partner, Perdita, to kill Sailor. When Sailor arrives at Big Tuna, the town in which Perdita lives, she lies to him, telling him that she has heard of no contract. Soon after, Sailor meets Bobby Peru, a man who pretends to befriend Sailor and even offer him an easy job robbing a feed store. It turns out, however, that Peru is in cahoots with Perdita.

This collapse of the distinction between form and reality is diametrically opposed to the sweet relationships of transcendental irony. In the realm of deception, one fixates on one form as the representative of the real. He thus becomes blind to the possibility that this representation, like all representations, can only partially reveal reality, that reality is ultimately ungraspable. The victim of deception, such as Sailor in relation to Perdita, blinds himself to the film's key question: what thrives in the gap between form and reality? This victim assumes for an instant that no gap exists, that this form—Perdita's performance, for instance—accurately reveals this reality—Perdita's intended meaning, for example. In closing this gap between form and reality, this victim actually widens the distance between reality and form. Fixating on this single pattern as a revealer of truth, reducing the real to one representation, the victim actually ends up losing the real, for he cuts away the ungraspable energy of the real, its powers always beyond disclosure. Hungry for reality, he divorces himself from reality. Wishing to avoid deception, he becomes hopelessly deceived.

In contrast, the ironist never reduces reality to one form. He remains open to the possibility that no one form can ever capture the real. He knows that reality is ungraspable, beyond full disclosure. The practitioner of irony is always attuned to his primary assumption: a gap always exists between the stable pattern and unstable reality. This practitioner is thus like Sailor before he falls into the simple faith of deception's victim. That is, this practitioner of irony resembles the Sailor who understands that his passion for Lula can never be represented by any one form of affection, who attempts to realize his love in an array of forms, ranging from wild lovemaking to turbulent dancing to boisterous speech. In holding open the gap between reality and form, this practitioner ironically comes close to the real. Open to numerous forms as partial revealers of truth, he approximates the unstable, inexhaustible nature of the real. He opens himself to a familiar marriage with the strange, to intimate knowledge of the transcendent, to gnosis. Accepting the divide between form and reality, he closes the gap between the two. Knowing that all forms are deceptions, he is never really deceived.

The Death of Love

Upon arriving in Big Tuna, Sailor and Lula both lose their irony, the ability to play in the sweet gap between reality and form. They quickly become victims to one of Marietta's pawns, Bobby Peru. Falling victim to deception, they almost immediately lose their intimacy, their *amor*. In almost no time, their dimly lighted, self-contained bower of love becomes exposed to harsh light from the desert, and their feeling of timeless separation from the world becomes constrained to a relentless schedule for separate actions.

As mentioned, Sailor believes Perdita when she tells him that there is no contract out on him. He thus thinks that Bobby Peru is a slightly sinister though mostly affable small-time criminal who ultimately has his best interests at heart. After Bobby has just come from violating Lula, he drives over to where Sailor is changing the oil in his car and asks Sailor if he'd like to have a beer. Looking at his watch—for the first time in the film—Sailor says yes, and the two men soon after find themselves several beers into a conversation at a local bar. Bobby pretends concern for Sailor's financial welfare. He invites Sailor to join him in an easy robbery job at a nearby feed store. The money gleaned from the robbery, Bobby claims, will help Sailor and Lula make their way to California or elsewhere. Sailor agrees. As the Wicked Witch as Marietta watches in her crystal ball, Sailor claims that this extra money could help him and Lula get further down the yellow brick road. He clearly in this case sees Bobby as a helpful guide.

However, only minutes before seeing Sailor, Bobby has subtly violated Lula. In this complex scene, Bobby begins by violently accosting Lula but ends by seducing her—that is, by deceiving her into believing that his designs are legitimately erotic. Bobby abruptly enters Lula's room at a Big Tuna motel—her bower of love is no longer impervious to the outside world. He says he needs to "go to the head," a reference already charged with vulgar sexuality. When he finishes urinating—he does so loudly and with the door to the bathroom open—he walks into the room and immediately begins making lewd remarks to Lula, claiming that she likes to "fuck like a bunny," that she wants to "fuck Bobby Peru." When she tells him to leave, he brutally grabs her neck, touches her breast, and caresses her crotch. He then says he'll leave if she'll only say "fuck me." As he whispers the words in her ears over and over, Lula becomes increasingly aroused. Just when she verges on reaching climax, she gives into to Bobby's request: she says, seductively, "fuck me." She at this point believes that Bobby desires her erotically. She shares this desire. However, right after she says what Bobby wants, he abruptly pulls back and states that he can't do what she wants right now. He'll have to later, he claims. He then leaves. Lula has allowed herself to be deceived by Bobby. She has taken seriously his brutal though vacuous form of eroticism.

In allowing themselves to be deceived by Bobby, Sailor and Lula betray one another. Thinking of his criminal past, Sailor had promised Lula earlier that he would never again do anything without a "good reason." In agreeing to rob a feed store, he breaks this promise. When he returns to Lula after drinking beers with Bobby and she asks him what he's been up to, he chooses not to tell her about his planned caper. For the first time in the film, he tells an outright lie to his lover. Doing so, he breaks the primary code of *amor*—faithfulness to the sacred beloved.

Lula likewise breaks this code. Earlier in the film, she had promised Sailor that she'd always be true to him, that she'd stand by him, that she'd go to the "ends of the earth for him." In giving over to Bobby's seductions, she violates her promise. When Sailor returns to their hotel room after being with Bobby, she doesn't tell Sailor about Bobby's earlier visit. This silence essentially constitutes a lie, an attempt to cover up the way things are. Lula breaches her amorous contract with Sailor. She distances herself from his affection. She chooses the evil demiurge over her possible salvation.

The respective deceptions of Sailor and Lula correspond to several signs of their demise. First of all, both Sailor and Lula in Big Tuna find themselves controlled by time. Once Sailor and Lula reach Big Tuna, Sailor on two occasions looks at his watch—when Bobby asks him if he wants a beer and when he waits for Bobby to pick him up for the robbery. He is now a subject of temporality. He is no longer able to enclose himself in a bower of love seemingly separate from the world's inevitable decay. Likewise, Lula, soon after reaching Big Tuna, discovers that she, too, is now a victim of temporality. During her first day in this wasted town, she vomits on the floor of her motel room. She quickly finds out why: she's pregnant, and thus now caught in an inexorable nine-month cycle that will end in painful labor. A second sign of Sailor and Lula's descent is their motel room. Unlike their other dimly illuminated, self-contained abodes, this one is harshly lighted and pervious to outside scenes. Even the blinds of the room don't block the Texas glare, and the door doesn't shut out the vulgar sounds of the set of a "pornographical film" being shot in an adjoining room. Yet a third token of the fall of these lovers is the actual vomit on the floor of the motel room. The opening shot of this room features flies buzzing around Lula's vomit. Death and nausea have invaded the sweet love of Sailor and Lula. They are now immured to excrement of the foulest sort.[14] A fourth sign of the demise of Sailor and Lula is absence of their shared fire. Now when the two light up to smoke, we no longer witness the single cigarette bursting into flame. We watch each smoke separately, alone.

Lula acknowledges her growing distance from Sailor by admitting to him that she's not sure that she wants to have their baby. She assures him that she loves him, but questions their future together. She fears that they have somehow gotten away from the yellow brick road, that they are now threatened on all sides by the Wicked Witch. It appears that the embryo growing inside of her is more a sign of despair than of hope, a sign of their fall into generation. They can no longer say that their love is perfect and timeless. It has descended into procreation and thus into the labor of existence.

The Logic of Romance

This fall is consummated quickly. Sailor goes out on the robbery job with Bobby. Violating his promise that no one will get hurt, Bobby shoots the two cashiers of the feed store and then turns his weapon onto Sailor. His identity and intention become clear—he is one of Marietta's pawns and he means to murder Sailor. Sailor escapes this attempt on his life—Bobby finds that he is out of ammunition and is soon after this discovery shot by the police— but is caught by the law. While Sailor languishes in a Texas jail, Lula waits in the lobby of the jailhouse. Her mother appears along with Santos and tells Lula that she must return home. Lula claims that she can't forsake Sailor. Marietta reiterates her desire and Santos embraces Lula in a hug that is more an imprisoning hold than a sign of affection. Trapped in the arms of her nemesis, Lula screams loudly.

The film doesn't end here, though, even though "reality" might suggest that it should. It seems clear at this point that Sailor and Lula are dangerously disconnected. Not only is their relationship troubled by mutual deception; they are also on the verge of being separated for the five years of Sailor's prison term. Moreover, Lula is once more immured in the lair of Marietta, her enemy, and Sailor, once released, will be an easy target for Santos's hit men. The situation seems thoroughly hopeless. Any honest director, one would think, would realize this bleak situation and simply end his picture with Lula and Sailor miles apart, with Lula in the arms of Santos and Sailor in a Texas jail.

However, Lynch rebels against these "realist" conventions. His film, recall, is devoted to romance, a genre that requires a "happy" ending.[15] Unlike the realist genre, which requires fealty to the painful limitations of space and time, the romance genre encourages commitment to the total satisfactions of *amor*— desire utterly fulfilled, fear entirely assuaged. Though this satisfaction might not occur in the so-called "real" life of the empirical world, it remains nonetheless an ideal of redemption, a paragon of salvation. Impossible in the everyday plane of fear and desire, of deception and violence, this romantic transcendence of empirical limitation must exist in artifice—in the aesthetic realms of courtliness, of dance, and, of course, of movies. In providing an eminently satisfying ending to his film, an ending replete with obvious cinematic allusions, Lynch is showing his devotion to the transcendental possibilities of romance: to the idea that the blissful conclusion is healing, holistic, hovering above temporal anguish.

Lynch's happy ending ignores the more vexed conclusion to Gifford's novel. In the book, Sailor and Lula separate at the end; their romance is over, and they go down different paths. In Lynch's film, the two characters recover their perfect unity; their romance is rekindled, and marriage appears to be in their near future. Sailor after almost six years is released from prison. Lula's mother calls her daughter and begs her not to reunite with Sailor. Lula in anger tosses her drink on a photograph of Marietta. The picture begins to steam and fade away—the Wicked Witch, it appears, is melting away. Dorothy is on the verge of having her wish fulfilled. She will soon get to return to her true home, the place in which all of her wishes come true—the tender arms of her beloved. With her and Sailor's son Pace—his name means peace—she drives to the train station where Sailor awaits her. After a brief conversation, Sailor concludes that this reunion is awkward, that it's all wrong. He walks away. Lula weeps as he goes. When he is several hundred yards away from Lula, Sailor finds himself in a highly unlikely situation; he confronts several street toughs. He insults them and is quickly beaten down. While he lies unconscious, the Good Witch of the North (Sheryl Lee) appears to him in a vision. She delivers a sermon on the powers of romantic love and encourages Sailor to return to Lula at once. Sailor awakens from his stupor, apologizes to the thugs, and runs to Lula. He finds her, along with their son, in a car stranded in traffic because of a terrible accident. There, in the midst of polluting fumes and bloody wreckage, he proclaims to Lula his everlasting love and breaks into a rendition of Elvis's "Love Me Tender," a song that he has all of his life been saving for his wife. He and Lula have risen above the ruinous fray. Their *amor* has saved them from deadening divorce and promises them vital harmony.

Audience members undoubtedly enjoy the same satisfaction of Lula and Sailor. In ending his film with citations of *The Wizard of Oz* and Elvis musicals, Lynch recalls for viewers Hollywood's most artificially blissful pictures, those films that are entirely untroubled by the trammels of space and time. Such movies are in the end romances, for they are interested only in what makes audiences happy, in what allows viewers for a moment to escape the anguished pressures of their daily grinds. Though such movies might seem to be escapist trifles, they are in fact salves for the hurt soul, Gnostic rebellions against the vicious rigors of matter.[16]

The Hollywood Ending

But let's face it: we really can't take *Wild at Heart* that seriously as a mode of redemption.[17] Indeed, the film throughout seems to be but a parody of other films—of earlier Hollywood movies and of

Lynch's pictures themselves. Serving basically as parody, the movie is nothing more than a series of mocking citations of other motion pictures.[18] *Wild at Heart* lacks precisely a heart. It is essentially a sequence of forms without any real content; it is more or less a parade of mere surfaces behind which is no significant depth. The movie doesn't redeem so much as divert; it is not a romance as much as it is a send-up. If the film does indeed invoke romantic love, it does so only to make fun of Hollywood versions of affection. The film, in the end, seems to suggest that real love is impossible—only fake love, artificial movie love, can exist.

The primary victims of Lynch's satirical wit are *The Wizard of Oz* and Elvis films. Of course, as noted, the movie's basic structure is modeled on the plot of *The Wizard of Oz*. Lula, like Dorothy, makes her way down the yellow brick road in hopes of discovering her true home, her true romance with Sailor. Along the way she is hounded by her mother, a figure for the Wicked Witch. Just when it appears that Lula will never find Oz, will never find the means to return to her Sailor, Glinda the Good Witch literally appears to Sailor in a vision and encourages him to stay with Lula no matter what. Surely, on one level, these citations of *The Wizard of Oz* are just plain ridiculous. They take away from the movie's violent seriousness, from its delvings into the psychology of love. On another level, these citations work to mock the optimism of *The Wizard of Oz*, its smarmy belief in happy endings. In emphasizing the older film's hopeful ebullience in an unbelievable deus ex machina, *Wild at Heart* reveals the total artifice of Hollywood joy.

The Elvis allusions work in the same way as the ones from *The Wizard of Oz*: they detract from the seriousness of *Wild at Heart* and undercut the film's ostensible efforts to depict a legitimate transformation in Sailor. Sailor, like Lula, is but a cipher for a Hollywood figure of yore. Where Lula is only Dorothy returned, Sailor is Elvis again on the prowl. Though the name "Elvis" is never once mentioned in the movie, Sailor is obviously an Elvis impersonator. He features jet-black hair like the King. He talks like Elvis. He breaks into Elvis songs on two occasions. He casts himself as a young rebel. An amalgamation of stereotypical Elvis ticks, Sailor is ultimately something of a buffoon, more a character offering comic relief than a lover in question of salvation. In casting Sailor as a clown, the film implicitly suggests that Elvis, too, is silly, and further intimates that his movies are likewise ridiculous renderings of the artifice of Hollywood affection.

Lynch in *Wild at Heart* even appears to parody his own past cinematic sensibilities. For instance, the perverse violence preceding Johnny Farragut's murder—a blending of sexual desire and lust for death—resembles the violence that Frank perpetrates on Jeffrey in *Blue Velvet*, likewise a bizarre merging of erotic passion and brutal assault. Likewise, Lula's endless visions of Oz recall Sandy's dream of the robins in *Blue Velvet*; in both cases, a young, innocent girl tries to envision a better world where there is no pain. Finally, the pervasive weirdness of Mr. Reindeer's atmosphere—replete with topless girls dancing for him while he defecates and outlandish circus acts entertaining him during dinner—recalls that stereotypical Lynchian "strangeness" present in several of Lynch's movies: *Eraserhead* with its bizarre woman in the radiator, *Blue Velvet* with its sadomasochism and nitrous oxide, *Dune* with its languorous worms and blood-sucking Harkonnens. In citing his earlier films directly or indirectly, Lynch suggests that he's more interested in creating a "Lynch" film than in fashioning a meaningful cinematic event. Parodying himself, he undercuts the value of his movie.

As was the case in *Eraserhead* and *Blue Velvet*, Lynch in *Wild at Heart* has it both ways. On the one hand, he features a serious film on the redemptive virtues of *amor*. On the other hand, he renders a silly movie that is an exercise in parody. The movie is a masterwork and a trifle, a psychology of romantic love and a pillaging of cinematic forms. It consumes itself, and in doing so leaves viewers in an interpretive limbo. Does this limbo suggest that romantic love is worthless, a way of experiencing the world that is not legitimate in the empirical realm? Or does this limbo intimate the exact opposite: romantic love pushes one to a third term beyond oppositions, to a harmony of energy and form? The answer to both of these questions is: yes. Yes, the film suggests that romantic love is a meaningless proposition, a vapid optimism in a fallen world. Yes, the film intimates that romantic love finds the ironic middle path between turbulence and pattern. In occupying both positions—in rejecting romantic love, in praising *amor*—the film in the end offers deep support for romantic love, an ironic interplay between boundless passion and comforting decorum. At once something and nothing, argument and erasure, Lynch's paean to *amor* ultimately shows that the most profound path to the sacred is through the strange corridors of paradox, the curious portals of self-consummation.

NOTES

1. Chris Rodley, ed., *Lynch on Lynch*, rev. ed. (New York: Faber & Faber, 2005), 193.

2. I frequently use the Latin *amor* throughout this chapter to distinguish this kind of love from *eros*—merely sexual love—and *caritas*—merely altruistic love. As I'll make clear in this chapter, *amor* falls between these kinds of love: it's erotic and charitable at the same time.

3. Michel Chion acutely observes that Sailor and Lula are "two touching live beings who are full of delicacy in the mutual relations, generally intelligent and sharp in their words" (*David Lynch* [London: British Film Institute, 1995], 137).

4. The champion of the "chaste love" argument is, according to Robert S. Briffault (*The Troubadours* [Bloomington: Indiana University Press, 1965], 103), Louis Gillet (*Dante* [Paris: Flammarion, 1941], 22). The exemplar of the "erotic love" school is Briffault. The champion of the third school is Joseph Campbell. He writes that "*amor* is neither of the right-hand path (the sublimating spirit, the mind and the community of man), nor of the indiscriminate left (the spontaneity of nature, the mutual incitement of the phallus and the womb), but is the path directly before one, of the eyes and their message to the heart" (*The Masks of God: Creative Mythology* [New York: Penguin, 1968], 177). In other words, for Campbell, *amor* is between chastity and eros. It occurs when the lover through his sensual embrace of a particular beloved achieves spiritual vision. This individual—this person, right here, right now, this body, right here, right now—is the path to the sacred spirit.

5. Briffault, *Troubadours*, 137–38; Kurt Rudolph, *Gnosis: The Nature and History of Gnosticism* (San Francisco: HarperSanFrancisco, 1987), 374–75; J. R. Haule, *Divine Madness* (Boston: Shambhala, 1990), 1–23.

6. Briffault, *Troubadours*, 138–39; Rudolph, *Gnosis*, 375–76; Georgi Vasilev, "Bogomills, Cathars, Lollards, and the High Social Position of Women During the Middles Ages," *Facta Universitatis* 2, no. 7 (2000): 325–36,

http://facta.junis.ni.ac.yu/facta/pas/pas2000/pas2000-02.pdf; Haule, *Divine Madness*, 1–23.

7. Briffault, *Troubadours*, 26–28; Haule, *Divine Madness*, 1–23.

8. Ibid.

9. Even though Campbell rejects the Gnostic influence on the troubadours, this is his basic idea (*Masks of God*, 177).

10. Salmon Rushdie famously reads against this grain. He maintains that *The Wizard of Oz* is about the quest to leave home (*The Wizard of Oz* [London: British Film Institute, 1992], 9–11).

11. Martha P. Nochimson claims that Marietta's motherhood is a "dangerous rage-to-control directed at Lula" (*The Passion of David Lynch: Wild at Heart in Hollywood* [Austin: University of Texas Press, 1997], 49).

12. John Alexander helpfully makes this point. The destructive fire of Marietta is countered by the passionate fire of Sailor and Lula, generally symbolized by their postcoital cigarettes. He even comes up with a sort of register to mark the two characters' level of intimacy: "a single match, a single cigarette—Sailor's individuality; one match, two cigarettes—unity; sharing the same cigarette—intimacy" (*The Films of David Lynch* [London: Charles Letts, 1993], 113).

13. Chion concisely describes this concord: Sailor's and Lula's "mutual understanding is . . . harmonious and idealised" (*David Lynch*, 127).

14. Devin McKinney highlights the power of these and other extremely offensive images in the film. Lynch's "methods of offending the audience," he claims, "come, in various measures, out of Dada, the theatre of cruelty, Abstract Expressionism (form subsuming content), and 'the poetic cinema of shock'" ("Review of *Wild at Heart*," *Film Quarterly* 45, no. 2 [Winter 1991–92]: 42).

15. Northrop Frye wrote that interest in literature (and, by extension, film) tends "to center either in the area of tragedy, realism, and irony, or in the area of comedy and romance." Those attuned to the former sort of literature hope that the text will yield a serious truth, a useful criticism of life, or an ennobling moral. Readers interested in the latter type are keen on uncritical enjoyment of a story—the pleasurable conventions of set forms, the joy of aesthetic closure. If enjoyment of the first literary form requires a sophisticated, somewhat jaded outlook on life, a sense of fragmentation, then appreciation of the second kind of literature emerges from a primitive hope that concord wins out over discord, boy and girl in the end fall into each other's arms.

16. Nochimson believes that this ending is legitimate, that it shows Sailor transcending his limitations and becoming a "seeker" and that it depicts Lula "moving beyond the traditional controls on her" and attaining "the power of a secret bearer of major importance" (*Passion of David Lynch*, 146). She further claims that Lynch's use of popular culture icons at the end of his film "celebrates the collective unconscious that selects its own icons on its own

terms from what the power structure of Hollywood proposes" (ibid., 50). Of course, I here partially disagree with Nochimson—I maintain that Lynch "means" his happy ending but "unmeans" it as well.

17. Indeed, Rodley claims that "the film fails to achieve [Lynch's] usual perfect synthesis of the extremes of dark and light; humour and dread" (*Lynch on Lynch*, 192). Kathleen Murphy agrees, claiming that the film offers only "trivial thrills, cheapjack spooks and mysteries." Indeed, to Murphy the picture is "very like a *Saturday Night Live* spoof of Lynchland" ("Dead Heat on a Merry-Go-Round," *Film Comment* 26, no. 6 [November 1990]: 60).

18. Michael Dunne calls Lynch's mixing of parodies Bakhtinian. He claims that Lynch's film features a dialogic model, based on the "assumption that all utterances engage in dialogue with other utterances, present and absent, and that, furthermore, all of the possible utterances carry traces of their former social contexts" ("*Wild at Heart* in Three Ways: Lynch, Gifford, Bahktin," *Literature/Film Quarterly* 23, no. 1 [1995]: 6). Of course, a corollary of this Bahktinian argument is that voices might well be simply parodying other voices.

CHAPTER FOUR

Positive Negation in *Lost Highway*

Luminous Gloom

When asked about the inspiration behind *Lost Highway*, Lynch claimed that meditation can often lead to a film's major ideas. In practicing this kind of meditation, one simply starts thinking and then allows one idea spontaneously to generate another. After a while, once numerous ideas have been produced, one even forgets the starting point. Occasionally, one becomes so consumed by the ideas that he actually loses sight of the fact that he is thinking at all. His identity is swallowed up in the thought. He has turned inseparable from his thought. He is one with his thinking. In this state, according to Lynch, one is "lost," forsaken of self, bewildered. Yet, if one can endure this confusion, then from time to time he might "suddenly drop through a trapdoor into the big idea bank." Then this contemplative soul will have "a thing happening"—a major vision.[1]

Hidden in Lynch's statements on meditation is this paradoxical idea: only by being lost, by being taken up into outlandish ideas, can one be found, be blessed with a glimpse into the enduring archetype. This unsettling idea is based on a theory of negation. In negating clarity, in annihilating a sense of purpose, one discovers a deep lucidity, a connection to an ultimate end. This negation constitutes a strange sort of quest, a seeking for truth grounded on ignorance, a reconnaissance for light controlled by utter darkness. Such a quest requires us to reverse our traditional expectations. Instead of assuming that small insights lead to the great glimpse, one must believe that large confusion concludes in sacred vision. One can only know God, for instance, in being totally ignorant of God's being. One can only find one's direction in life, for example, by riding endlessly on the lost highway. These reversals indeed encourage us to reconsider Lynch's own *Lost Highway*, an ostensibly nihilistic vision, as a found road, a path to salvation.

Lynch's *Lost Highway* appears to be a manifestation of an ancient theological tradition: the *apophatic* tradition, the tradition devoted to negative theology. This theological current, akin to Gnosticism, maintains that God is so radically transcendent that he can only be known through what he is *not*. As opposed to the *kataphatic* tradition, based on a positive notion that God can actually be understood through what he *is*, negative theology maintains that God is ultimately unknowable in earthly terms. In this view, any attempt to corral God in human concepts is blasphemous, a reduction of the otherworldly to the worldly, the sacred to the profane. The only path to God is through ignorance, the negation of all ordinary knowing. Annihilating mundane understanding, becoming lost to the world, one finds himself in a position to gain supra-mundane acquaintance, gnosis of the spirit beyond this visible universe.

This tradition of negative theology has its roots in Gnosticism and Neoplatonism. Despite a clear difference between these schools of thought—Gnostics maintained that matter is separate from God while Neoplatonists held that matter is a reflection of divinity—both believed that the Godhead is radically transcendent and thus beyond human representation. Given this utter "otherness" of God, the only way to discourse of this being is through negation, through speaking of God only insofar as he is not one thing or another—not good, not just, not beautiful, not even a being. In the fifth century, Dionysius the Areopagite, also known as Pseudo-Dionysius, makes these Gnostics and Neoplatonic currents the basis for a full-fledged theology of negation.

Inflecting this basic idea—reality can only be experienced through an immediate identification with negation—*Lost Highway* shares with Lynch's other ironic pictures an emphasis on the value of raw, prelinguistic contact with life's great mystery. Like *Eraserhead*, *Blue Velvet*, and *Wild at Heart*, Lynch's 1997 film is skeptical toward idea, toward conceptual representation. As with its predecessors, this latter picture believes indeed that intellectual systems and the words that manifest them alienate one from the real. Only by renouncing rational control, only by losing oneself in particulars, can one find the strange core of existence, the radiant center that connects one to the cosmos.[2]

Lost Highway places no credence in positive conception. Indeed, the movie is ultimately a study in *emptiness*, in the curious idea that one can touch the Great Thing only as No-Thing. Espousing this latter idea, *Lost Highway* reaches the weird nihilistic essence of the Gnostic tradition, the notion that belief in absolutely nothing might result in a shattering experience of absolutely everything. In doing so, this movie finds itself on the outré margins of religious experience, based on the unsettling, barely conceivable notion that total ignorance is the precursor to holy knowledge.

In *Lost Highway*, the protagonist Fred Madison (Bill Pullman) spends the first half of the picture longing for total knowledge, for omnipotence. This quest for full knowing ironically alienates him from self-knowledge. In unrealistically wishing to understand everything, he blinds himself to what is most apparent. He is a monomaniacal solipsist, a man so obsessed with a desire to observe and control his environment that he can only witness his own perceptions and memories and not actual things and events. He is unable to understand the mystery of reality, to grasp the role of a Mystery Man (Robert Blake) that continually tries to remind him of his brutal narcissism. Only when his compulsive narcissism annihilates his environment entirely does he begin to purge his desire to know everything. He finds himself in a self-induced prison where he is literally cut off from everything else in the world, where all positive colors are negated to dull gray. In this chamber of utter negation and alienation, in this condition of confusion and lostness, Fred seems to find himself. He for the first time can imagine himself in another life, the life of one Pete Dayton (Balthazar Getty), in which he is charitable and open to otherness, attuned to things over perceptions, events over memories. However, Fred is unable to hold for long this vision. It seems that he is forever doomed to repeat the same round of solipsism, transcendence, and return to selfishness. *Lost Highway* appears to be a meditation on the difficulty of maintaining the negative way. Still, even though the movie is ostensibly about the failure of the negative way, there remains the hope, however faint, that one might at least for a time gain insight through negation, that he might break free of the alienating ego and connect with the cosmos.

The film's ambiguous form supports its ambiguous content. Indeed, the movie works to strip from viewers any positive interpretation. Through its use of shifting identities and strange doublings, vague insights and troubled gazes, the movie constantly leaves its audiences in doubt. We never quite know for sure if Fred really kills his wife Renee (Patricia Arquette) or if he simply imagines this murder. We never quite know for sure if Fred's alter ego, Pete Dayton, is a simple psychological projection of Fred or a real person. We are never really confident that we know who the Mystery Man is and what his function might be. These ambiguities— and there are numerous others—ensure that we will never quite rest in a conclusive interpretation, that we will forever remain in a hermeneutical limbo.

This troubling form is appropriate to negative theology. Stripping audiences of conclusive interpretations, of positive readings, this irreducible ambiguity forces viewers to face the negation of all knowing, the annihilation of significance. Thrown into this limbo of ignorance, viewers are, against expectation, opened to the mysterious darkness of truth, a truth too complex for the conceptions of human reason. Whether this truth lies in an utterly transcendent deity, in the curious human psyche, or in the strange core of this cosmos, it, this truth, must remain forever behind articulation, always hidden. Only by moving behind the barriers of words and thoughts, only by being hopelessly lost in the light, can one ever hope to find his way in the consuming darkness, the luminous gloom.

The Cloud of Unknowing

Though wildly heterogeneous, the Gnostics in general embraced the Platonic notion that the divine is irreducibly ineffable. Parts of the *Secret Book according to John* (c. 180 AD), a foundational Gnostic text, could almost have been written by Plato himself. For the anonymous author of this text, the true God is a radically transcendent power, an "immeasurable," "unfathomable," "unlimited," "invisible" void—a vast nothing. This mysterious "monad" cannot be conceived of in rational concepts or described in discursive language: "It is not corporeal, it is not *incorporeal*, it is not large, it is not small, it is *not* quantifiable, nor *is it* a *creature*. Indeed, no one can *think of it*."[3]

Plotinus, the fountainhead of Neoplatonism, attacked the Gnostics for their antimaterialism. In his *Enneads* (c. 250 AD), Plotinus criticizes the Gnostics for calling the demiurge, or worldmaker, evil. For Plotinus, the fashioner of the world is good, a valid emanation from the true deity. The true deity for Plotinus is the One, the origin and sustainer of the universe. This One is irreducibly ineffable. The only accurate way of speaking about this One is to say that nothing can be predicated of it, that it is "beyond all things and beyond the supreme majesty of the intellect." This means that we can only understand what this One is *not*—never what it *is*. The best way to approach this great negation of concepts is to "go away in silence and enquire no longer." However, this self-conscious silence, this refusal to question, does not mean that we can never have an inkling of the One's nature. On the contrary, when the intellect shuts down, another faculty takes over—the soul. When the soul becomes pure—that is, when it becomes entirely simple—then it no longer envisions the One as an object to be known. Instead, the purified soul resembles the One, identifies with the One, becomes like the One.[4]

Soon after the time when the Gnostics and the Neoplatonists were developing their negative theology, Christian thinkers were likewise developing the idea that one can only gain holy knowledge through ignorance. The most profound of these was Dionysius the Areopagite. Writing sometime in the sixth century, the Areopagite negates all concepts that could be conceivably applied to God, including wisdom, goodness, spirit, and paternity, including even nothingness, silence, and mystery. For the Areopagite, God is not only beyond all positive assertion—he is also outside the reach of negative statement. Practicing this radical negativity—this unwillingness to predicate anything at all of God—the religious seeker necessarily enters into a painful blindness, a difficult nonbelief. But this troublous condition is ultimately an *ekstasis*, an ecstasy, a transcendence of all earthly understanding to the divine darkness.[5]

Fred Madison's Positive Theology

Fred Madison, the protagonist of *Lost Highway*, is in the beginning consumed by a will to control the world with his own mind. This will to mastery inspires in Fred a desire to know the world only insofar as it fits his expectations. He is not ultimately interested in "reality" at all. Instead, he is passionate for fulfilling his own fantasies, his own solipsistic vision.[6] Such a passion of course inevitably blinds Fred to the real.[7] In hoping to know his environment as a reflection of himself, Fred ends up knowing nothing. Only by learning of his ignorance does he put himself in a position to understand anything. Fred is in serious need of negativity. He needs to divest himself of his narcissistic concepts, to annihilate his will to know. When he achieves this emptiness, he is for the first time ready to transcend his ego, to imagine a world in which he can be open to the real, charitably disposed toward the universe not as he wants it but as it is. In Fred's case, however, this openness is short-lived. His narrow ego quickly returns, and with it comes back the pain of solipsism, the agony of blocking objects with craven subjectivity.

Fairly early in the film, Fred's wife Renee reports to investigating detectives that Fred hates video cameras. When the police question Fred as to why he holds this view, he claims that he wants to know the world only as he remembers it, not as it really is. This split between subjective memory and objective fact runs throughout the film. In embracing solipsism, Fred necessarily divorces himself from empirical reality. However, this repressed empirical realm will not disappear. On the contrary, it continually haunts

Fred, disturbing his fantasies with fact. Though he desires to believe that he only wants to know the world as he perceives it, he in fact is consumed by a megalomaniac urge to understand the entire universe exactly as it is. This terrible rift in his own personality—a rift borne of two opposed modes of positive knowing, the subjective and the objective—causes in Fred an agonized existence.[8] He can only end this agony through negating his two urges toward positive knowledge. Cleansed of these desires to know, immersed in ignorance, he can open himself to the mystery of existence.

Renee and Fred must talk to the police for a bizarre reason. Renee has been finding on their front doorstep a single manila envelope. Inside of this envelope is a videocassette. When she and Fred play the cassette on the first morning Renee discovers the envelope, it features a black-and-white shot of the exterior of their home. Fred and Renee make nothing of the video; they assume it's from a real estate agent or something. The next morning that Renee finds the cassette, she and Fred watch in horror as the camera depicts the interior of their home and then actually pictures the couple sleeping. This last incident prompts Renee to call the police. She tells the cops that she and Fred live near the observatory. The police show up and soon realize that Fred hates video.

That Fred and Renee live near the observatory is significant. Though Fred appears to be shocked by the bizarre filming of his home's interiors, he in fact harbors an unconscious fantasy to be omniscient, to know the entire world fully, to survey his apartment even while he sleeps. We of course cannot conclude that Fred literally films himself and his wife sleeping. We can conclude, however, that this interior filming expresses a psychological fact— Fred unconsciously wishes to know everything, especially in relation to his wife. This later statement forces us to consider this troubling fact—*Lost Highway* is a "psychotopographic" landscape, an environment thoroughly imbued with Fred's psychological projections.[9] Most of the film appears to take place inside of Fred's head; each character appears to be a manifestation of his psyche, each place seems to be a reflection of his interiors. The true lost highway is Fred's soul.[10]

Certain clues lead to this conclusion, to this idea that the movie is a long interior dialogue, a conversation between two parts of one self, unknown to each other. An early scene establishes Fred's primary obsession: he jealously suspects his wife of infidelity. One night before he heads out to play a gig—he's a tenor saxophonist—Renee asks him if he's okay with her staying at home. He suspiciously asks her what she'll do in his absence. When she says she'll read, he repeats the word "read" twice in disbelief. After reaching his venue, Fred during a break between sets calls his home to check to see if Renee is there. The camera moves from room to room in Fred's house, revealing a ringing phone in every chamber. This overabundance of phones betrays Fred's true desire—to enjoy total omniscience so that he can monitor his wife's every move. Even though Fred later claims that he hates technologies that objectively reveal empirical reality, he obviously on an unconscious level wants nothing but a total view of the world.

This split between Fred's jealousy—a subjective position that sees the world only insofar as it relates to paranoia—and his hunger for omniscience—a potentially objective perspective that wants to see the world as it is, beyond any one ego—organizes the entire plotline of the first half of the movie. Indeed, the first half of the film seems entirely to be a reflection of this rift. Fred's conscious side is constantly engaging in jealous fantasies over his wife's infidelity. This jealousy, it appears, grows out of Fred's deep fear that his wife no longer loves him, no longer desires him. (In fact, in the only love scene between Fred and Renee, Fred is unable to perform.) Insecure over her affection for him, he assumes that she longs for other men. This is of course the psychology behind Fred's jealousy: he loathes himself for his insecurity and thus assumes that his wife loathes him as well; he doesn't trust himself and therefore doesn't trust his wife, either. This mixture of fear and distrust ensures that Fred's perceptions will necessarily be clouded. Whenever the jealous Fred sees Renee, he perceives her neglecting him for another; whenever the jealous Fred cannot see Renee, he envisions her imagined infidelity with eerie precision. In both cases, he lives only within his own narrow perspective borne of obsessive fear and paranoia. Consumed by an illusory life—one supported by his playing sax in a cacophonous, surreal style; by his spending endless hours in a soundproof practice room; and by his living in a house devoid of natural light—Fred cannot understand that the part of himself that is not drawn to delusion, that violent part of himself that wants to know and to possess at any cost what he cannot fully understand or have, wants, ultimately, to kill his wife if he cannot have total knowledge of and control over her. This aspect of Fred's psyche is likely what is behind the nightly videos of the house, efforts to watch and record the activities of his evasive wife. This element of Fred's psychic composition is also behind the strange Mystery Man whom Fred first meets at a party of one of Renee's alleged suitors. This man, like Fred, appears to be able to be in two places at once, at both the party and Fred's house. This part of Fred's mind is moreover behind the climactic event in the film, the alleged murder of Renee. This murder takes place entirely beyond Fred's waking consciousness. Fred simply wakes up one morning, picks up the daily video, and then sees on the television screen the gruesome act.

Fred's split personality is most clearly manifested in these latter two scenes—the scene at the party of Renee's ostensible suitor and the murder scene. At a party thrown by a man named Andy (Michael Massee), Fred is extremely jealous and quite drunk. Renee is especially friendly with Andy, so Fred naturally assumes that she's having an affair. Upset over this possibility, he throws back neat scotches while he watches his wife's every move. While he is engaged in this fearful act of paranoia—an act doomed to produce delusion—he enters into a conversation with a strange and nameless man. This man simply appears at the party. He wears a black robe and features a face covered in white makeup. He wears lipstick. He walks directly up to Fred and begins to talk to him. The music at the party fades. All we hear are the voices of Fred and the Mystery Man. The Mystery Man claims that he and Fred have met before. Fred denies the meeting. The Mystery Man then says that he's at Fred's home at this very instant. To prove his point, he takes out a mobile phone and demands that Fred call his home. Fred does so, and the Mystery Man actually answers the phone. He's in two places at once; he's ubiquitous; he is seemingly omniscient. When a disturbed Fred asks why the man is in his house, the man simply answers that it's not his "custom" to go where he's not invited. The implication is clear: though he doesn't know this, Fred has welcomed this presence into his house because this presence is a part of his very self. It is the part that watches and records the exteriors and interiors of his home. It is that part that wants to watch his wife's every move, that wants to dominate her, to control her, to kill her.

Fred rushes Renee out of the party and returns home. As he approaches the driveway, he thinks he witnesses a presence in his home. Of course he does—he sees that part of himself that is embodied by the Mystery Man. He enters his house alone, looking for the intruder. He finds nothing. Renee enters the house. While she removes her makeup and prepares to go to bed, Fred wanders in and out of the shadows of his labyrinthine house, a house that reflects his own convoluted mind. At one point, he enters fully into what appears to be a totally dark chamber. When Renee calls out for him, he doesn't answer. He has clearly merged with the presence in his house, lost his identity in a dark urge to control and kill. After Renee has gone to bed, he emerges again from the shadows. The camera cuts to the next morning. Fred walks outside and retrieves the single manila envelope. He watches the video inside. It features a shot of his house's exterior and then of his home's interiors and then of him in his bedroom covered in blood and screaming beside Renee's mutilated corpse. Immediately, he is punched in the nose by one of the cops who earlier visited his home. This detective, like the videos, like the Mystery Man, has simply appeared out of nowhere. This policeman, like most everything else, is clearly but another manifestation of Fred's tortured psyche.

One could almost work out an allegory of the film's first part, assigning every character a place in Fred's psyche. In this allegory, Fred's character itself would be Fred's conscious awareness, that part of him that wishes to reduce the world to solipsistic desire. The Mystery Man would be Fred's unconscious, the aspect of his psyche that wants total knowledge of and control over the world.[11] Andy, Fred's rival, would be a manifestation of his paranoia, his jealous fear that the entire world is out to steal his beloved. The detectives would of course reflect Fred's guilt over wanting to dominate and possibly murder his environment. The only character who appears to exist beyond Fred's psyche is Renee, who seems to represent the Real, the Unknown, the Ultimate Mystery. She is Fred's great desideratum, the sacred power that he most wants to possess. However, because he wishes to possess this power—wishes to reduce it to his subjective ego or dominate it with his objective reason—he actually divorces himself from it. In attempting to flatten Renee to a narcissistic perception—into a reflection of his ego—he necessarily knows only those parts of her that correspond to his own selfish desires. In trying to know and control Renee thoroughly—to dominate her every move—he inevitably kills her and thus loses the object of knowledge.[12]

That the first half of the film is controlled by Fred's psyche is apt. Consumed by a positive desire to reduce the world to his subjectivity or to know the world through objective faculties, he is doomed to impose his will onto the Real—his will to power, his will to know. Though he exerts this will in the name of knowing, he actually ensures that he will *not* know the world, that he will fit the mysterious Real into his human grids. If Fred is ever to understand Renee as the Real, he will have to go through a negative movement. He will have to renounce his urges to flatten the Real to his ready-made grids. He will have to hover in the void, in the nothing, before he can find anything. He will have to take a long and harrowing ride on the lost highway before he discovers the road.

The Failed Quest for the Real

This negation occurs in the scene following Fred's alleged murder of Renee. (I say "alleged" because it's entirely possible that he really did murder his wife. As I've noted, it is impossible to tell what is dream and what is reality in this film. I'll return to this point later.) In contrast to the many earlier scenes that feature Fred looking down on the world through the windows in his second-story house—that feature him in his makeshift observatory—the first shot after Fred is convicted of murder (by himself? by the police?) shows him walking down stairs to a dark, windowless death row. Whether Fred is imagining this imprisonment or whether it's real is finally immaterial. The point is this: Fred is now in a realm stripped of color and light, of significance and purpose. His prison uniform is drab gray. His cell is drab gray. The area in which he takes recreation is drab gray. Fred moves through this gloomy monotone with no other agenda than breathing and eating. He can have nothing to look forward to, nothing to interpret, nothing on which to impose his mind. He is in limbo, a meaningless emptiness between blind past and a future of annihilation. In this nihilistic region, what can Fred do but dissolve his ego into nothing in particular? But this dissolution need not be merely negative. It could well be a fundamental destruction out of which a new creation might grow, a melancholy bewilderment that lays the ground for ecstatic transcendence.

The key question is this: is this empty environment a manifestation of Fred's mind, or is it merely a prison in which he suddenly finds himself? Put another way, is Fred actively seeking to negate his past positive methods of knowing, or is he simply suffering confusion over his alleged murder of his wife? If we read the film so far as a psychotopographic panorama, then we can conclude that Fred has actually willed himself to become will-less, that he has actively relinquished his past modes of knowing and thus become a passive observer of the world, a man reticent to impose his will on the mystery of it all. He has seen his former way of understanding the world fail miserably. He has realized that this mode leads only to alienation—from self and others—and murder—of others, of self. Armed with this insight, he can only choose to give up his narrow ego and his rapacious reason. Throwing these elements to the side, he hovers in a weird void. This is the no-thing of negative theology, the darkness that might lead to the light.

This languishing in the abyss is extremely painful. Very soon after he is incarcerated, Fred experiences excruciating headaches. These pains are beyond the help of any mere doctor. They are the psychic agonies born of divorcing oneself from the realm of familiar things and throwing oneself into the void. While undergoing these aches, Fred also suffers from another disturbance. He begins to have outlandish visions. He first witnesses a burning house in the desert. In reverse motion, as if time were turning back upon itself, the flames flow back into the home and disappear. The house itself, exploding in flames an instant earlier, returns to its normal state. The Mystery Man steps outside the door and stands ambiguously on the porch. Immediately following this bizarre sight, Fred witnesses another weird vision. He watches as what is ostensibly a car rushes quickly over a dark and lonely highway. The scene is eerie, chilling. Taken together, these two contiguous visions suggest this: Fred is now on the lost highway. The first part of the vision shows that Fred has reversed time to understand the cause of his violently destructive behavior. This cause is that part of himself figured by the Mystery Man, a presence that originates annihilating flames. Rejecting this presence and its murderous lights, Fred then turns to the second part of the vision: a dark road over which a bodiless eye quickly moves. This eye seemingly belongs to Fred. It is his haunted effort to witness the world without the aid of light or reason.

Along this visionary road, Fred rather quickly finds something: a young man standing alone on the shoulder. Soon after this sight, Fred actually *becomes* this young man. After undergoing an agonizing transformation in his cell, one that is violent and bloody, he awakens to find himself another man, Pete Dayton. One can of course read this stunning event literally and can thus conclude that a man on death row actually turns into someone else. Or, more interestingly, one can continue to read the film psychologically, and therefore opine that Fred through his negation of concepts has achieved an inner transformation, has metamorphosed into a new self, a supple and open and charitable self, the exact opposite of his former being—stiff, domineering, narcissistic. This latter reading, though far from definite, at least accounts for what happens in the second half of the film, a struggle between Fred's new self and the old Fred. Not surprisingly, this struggle centers on a woman who looks exactly like Renee, Alice Wakefield (also played by Patricia Arquette). She, like her double, figures a mysterious reality beyond conception.

The Negation of Fred

Pete Dayton is initially the exact opposite of Fred Madison.[13] As such, Pete constitutes a figure of transcendence—both a negation of Fred's former self and an affirmation of new being. Aptly, this new being at first practices a negative way. He opens himself to the mystery of existence without every attempting to impose his will on the world. Indeed, he is in his early stages something of a mystic, a man attuned to the weird beauty of life.

When Pete awakens in Fred's cell, he is understandably bewildered, as though he were an infant new to the world. Not only confused, he is also pained, for he suffers a nasty wound on his forehead. Far from debilitating Pete, this pained confusion serves as a positive negation, a power that holds at bay preconceived concepts and keeps the heart open to the holy strangeness of the universe. After Pete's parents escort him home from the prison, he retires to his backyard to rest. Near his white picket fence, he reclines in a red lounge chair. In contrast to the vampirelike Fred, a man who spends his days shut inside a dim home, Pete immediately seeks the outdoors, an experience of green grass and the wide blue sky. Soon, Pete rises from the chair and walks over to look at his neighbor's adjoining backyard. There he notices a dormant sprinkler, beside which stands a small brown-and-white terrier. Near the sprinkler and the dog is a small inflatable swimming pool. On its water floats a toy boat and a beach ball. Pete stands mesmerized before the scene, enraptured by the colors and the motions. He is like Adam coming to consciousness for the first time, utterly surprised by the world's curious freshness, its radiant emergences and its sweet rhythms.

This remarkable scene captures beautifully Pete's negative way. Though he is pained and confused, he does not defend himself against the potentially threatening world. Positioning himself under the abysmal sky and above the pulsating earth, he remains vulnerable to the unexpected. His suburban garden—his unfallen Eden—rewards his efforts. Within minutes, he experiences a vision of the disarming gorgeousness of the everyday, of colorful objects floating effortlessly on a surface of water. Aptly, this flexible, innocent soul is most drawn to buoyancy, to giving over to the currents and riding on the waves. In fact, in relinquishing his will to know, to control, he himself mimics the boat and the ball. He rests on the breath of life, contingent at every turn.

Lynch reinforces these meanings in a bit of clever intertextuality. The last time we saw a young man lounging in a backyard surrounded by a white picket fence was in *Blue Velvet*. Jeffrey Beaumont, recall, reclined in such an environment at the close of the film. His lounging, remember, suggested that he had become his father, a suburban patriarch bent on controlling nature with his hose, spade, and insecticide. Obviously, Pete is potentially a version of Jeffrey. He not only relaxes in the same way as his predecessor, he also associates himself with the implements that caused Jeffrey's father to have a stroke—a technology for watering a lawn (a sprinkler) and an animal capable of attacking the water (the terrier). But Pete in the end is the exact opposite of Jeffrey at *Blue Velvet*'s conclusion. Unlike Jeffrey at the film's close, Pete does not mimic his "father," Fred Madison. He does not attempt to manicure his experiences. On the contrary, he allows the turbulence to overtake him. For this refusal to exert his will to control, he is rewarded with something that will elude the father-loving Jeffrey: a witnessing of the mystery at the core of existence.

Early on, Pete features other qualities that display his negative way, his sensitivity to life's nuances and complexities. For instance, he is dubious of language, aware of the fact that words can never represent fully the strangeness of reality. Soon after he returns home, he and some friends go out for a good time. Among these friends is his girlfriend, Sheila (Natasha Gregson Wagner). At a certain point in the evening, she asks Pete if he still cares for her. Instead of answering, Pete simply gives her a long and passionate kiss on the lips.

The next day, Pete returns to work. He is a mechanic at a garage called Arnie's. As an ace mechanic, he must be especially attuned to the subtleties of physics. He displays this talent when one Mr. Eddy (Robert Loggia), a crime boss, brings in his Mercedes for a tune-up. Pete takes a ride with Mr. Eddy, listening all the while for disturbances in the motor. When he locates the disturbance, he tells Mr. Eddy to pull over. He lifts the hood and then delicately adjusts the engine with small, elegant tools.

A day later, Mr. Eddy returns in his Cadillac. He wishes to leave the car for a tune-up. Out of the car emerges a beautiful young woman. She looks exactly like Renee, except that she has blonde hair where Renee had black hair. As he earlier stood stunned before the floating boat and ball, Pete now stands mesmerized before this glorious woman. He does not impose his will or his words upon her. He simply allows her to be, to exist in her own right. This passivity draws the woman toward him. Later that evening, she returns to Arnie's alone. She walks to the threshold of the garage and gazes longingly at Pete. Pete shyly approaches her. She tells him her name—Alice Wakefield—and offers to go to dinner with him. After some hesitation—he fears that she is the girlfriend of the violent Mr. Eddy—he agrees to leave with her. They retire to a hotel room, where they make passionate love with one another.

In each of these cases, Pete, through his negation of his will to know and control, finds intimate unity with an external element—with Sheila, with a sophisticated motor, with Alice. Shunning Fred's egocentric paranoia, he features a keen sensitivity to nuance and complexity, an acute understanding of being. Through stepping back and releasing creatures to be what they are,[14] he grasps the subtle particularity of the things he beholds. He blinds himself so that he can see. He loses himself to discover his true home.

The Return of the Positive

Sadly, Pete's innocence is short-lived. Understandably, he finds it extremely difficult to suspend his ego, along with its fears and desires. He rather quickly reverts to Fred's modes of understanding the world. Indeed, it appears that his negation of Fred is doomed to a short life. Within days of his meeting Alice—seemingly a negation of Renee—he suffers from the same jealousy that beset Fred. In no time at all, Fred, along with the Mystery Man, returns. We realize that Pete constitutes a brief manifestation of an almost impossible negative way, a quick glimpse into what could be.

Like the double that she negates, Alice appears to stand for reality itself, the mysteriousness of the implacable world. Initially, Pete has no trouble at all connecting with her. In merging with her, he gains an expansive understanding of resplendent energies. Indeed, just before Alice first comes to Pete's garage, Lynch's camera lingers lovingly over the California sunset. This wide view—so refreshing

after the claustrophobic settings of Fred's life—establishes beautifully the appropriate context for Pete's beholding of Alice. In discovering sweet identity with her, he finds unity with the large and
marvelous cosmos. She is his portal to mystical participation.

But as soon as he finds Alice, he loses her. After only a few
meetings with Alice, Pete for good reasons begins to fear the violent jealousy of Mr. Eddy. Appearing as a proxy for the paranoid
Fred—all characters, recall, are likely manifestations of Fred's psyche—Mr. Eddy proves himself to be a tyrant, a man who must be
in control at all times.[15] Whatever he can't control, he beats or
kills. This habit of behavior is manifest in Mr. Eddy from the very
beginning. After Pete fixes the engine of his Mercedes, Mr. Eddy
decides to take a ride with Pete and his two henchmen. During
this ride, Mr. Eddy becomes incensed over a tailgating driver. After
allowing the driver to pass, Mr. Eddy viciously rams the driver
from behind and then runs him precipitously off the road. He
then violently pulls the man out of the car, brutally beats him, lec-
tures him on the rules of the road, and then makes him promise
to study the driver's manual. This display illustrates Mr. Eddy's
primary characteristic: he is a control freak, a man who must
always have things exactly as he wants them. Any deviance he
swiftly punishes.

Mr. Eddy, proxy for Fred's suspicious side, for his paranoia
and his jealousy, quickly takes over Pete's existence. In no time at
all, Pete begins to behave just like Mr. Eddy. He exhibits jealousy
and violence; he becomes tyrannical and criminal. Soon after
Alice informs Pete that Mr. Eddy might know of their love affair,
Pete turns jealous. He can't stand the idea of Alice being with
another man. Consumed with this desire to control Alice, he
loses his ability to apprehend the world as it is. Minutes after
Alice calls him one evening to say that she can't see him, he sits
alone in his room. As cacophonous Nine Inch Nails music plays
on the soundtrack, he notices an insect climbing up his wall and
then moths entrapped in his overhead light fixture. Whereas he
earlier might have marveled at the individuality of these creatures, he is here troubled by their crawling and flying. He finds
them annoying and abruptly leaves his house. Angry over the
recalcitrant otherness of the world, he picks up Sheila, his old

girlfriend, and brutally makes love to her. He has lost his sensitivity and compassion. He simply uses Sheila to satisfy his lust. Soon after, he surreptitiously meets Alice. She tells him that Mr. Eddy will kill them if they don't leave town. During the course of the conversation, Alice narrates her history with Mr. Eddy. In the form of a flashback, Lynch shows this sordid tale of sex and violence—during which we learn that Alice is basically an actress in Mr. Eddy's porno movies. In the midst of this depiction, Alice is forced at gunpoint to strip for Mr. Eddy. After removing everything but her panties, she walks lustily toward Mr. Eddy, goes to her knees before him, and then touches his face. When Lynch returns to the present scene, Alice talking to Pete in a hotel room, he cuts in such a way that Alice touches Pete's face in the same fashion in which she earlier touched Mr. Eddy's face. Pete is becoming Mr. Eddy. This parallel is borne out even more strongly minutes later, when Alice convinces Pete to help her rob Andy—the same Andy that Fred formerly loathed. In completing this task, Pete will become a full double of the criminal Mr. Eddy.

In turning into Mr. Eddy, Pete of course is really transforming back into Fred. As I mentioned earlier, Mr. Eddy is but a manifestation of Fred's violent and jealous side. After taking on these traits, Pete precipitously becomes Fred. After robbing (and accidentally killing) Andy, Pete and Alice take off in a red convertible with a black top, a car very similar to Fred's car of the same two colors. As they make their way down the highway, we witness what Fred earlier saw in his prison vision: the dark road eerily rushing under a quickly moving car. Alice then tells Pete that they need to drive to the desert to meet with a "fence," a person who can give them passports for the jewels they have stolen. The house in which this "fence" lives is the exact same house that Fred witnessed during his prison vision.[16] As Alice tells Pete of this house, it once more metamorphoses, through reverse photography, from a burning mess to an intact structure with the Mystery Man standing portentously on the porch. When Alice and Pete arrive at the house, no one is home. While Pete and Alice wait, they start making love in the sand. The music in the background, the ethereal "Song of the Siren" by This Mortal Coil, is the same that sounded when Fred earlier attempted to make love to Renee.

These parallels cease when Pete literally turns back into Fred. Just before Pete climaxes, Alice extricates herself from his embrace. The man to whom she was making love is no longer Pete but Fred. A naked Alice walks away from Fred and toward the house. As she disappears into the doorway, she mockingly says, "You can never have me." At this boundary between states, this "fence" between egocentrism and transcendence, self and other, history repeats itself: Fred, unable to negate his former self, unable to follow for long the *via negativa*, once more fails to merge with reality, again cannot consummate a relationship with the world. He finds himself all over again alone and in the dark. The feeble headlights of his car—all that cuts through the desert gloom—constitute an apt symbol of Fred's enduring consciousness: a measly pin light of perception in a vast abyss of mysterious life, a tiny ray of brightness blinding a man to the wonders of the cosmos.

Lost Highway reveals the difficulty of maintaining the negative way. Though Fred tries valiantly to negate his positive tyrannies, though he endeavors with all of his might to become Pete Dayton, a mystic of waves and water, of ships and spheres, he cannot hold to the abyss. The old hunger for meaning returns, the keen ache for some sort of graspable truth, for fact, for an anchor, for security. When this longing returns, it is but an instant before Fred's old demons come rushing back: his narcissistic ego, his need to narrow the world to his petty fears and desires, and his objective reason, his hope that he can discover, regardless of subjectivity, a lasting and durable truth.[17] Lynch's film, if anything, appears to be about the failure of the negative way, the impossible sacrifice required to achieve an absorption into the void. The movie seems to believe that even the best intentions toward negations are doomed to falter, that the old virus, the will to control, never really goes away. We might as well accept this, the picture opines, and thus embrace the saddest of situations: we are alone and alienated and violent.

The Failure of the Negative

Indeed, the minute Fred returns, so comes back the tyrannical violence. The Mystery Man appears on the porch of the house.

He carries a video camera, a manifestation of Fred's will to record the world objectively. Terrified, Fred drives away—he does not yet know himself well enough to realize that he's simply running from an integral part of his being. He drives to the same hotel where Pete and Alice once engaged in their assignations. There he realizes that Renee and Mr. Eddy, also known as Dick Laurent, are having sex in one of the rooms. Fred hides long enough to watch Renee leave. After she does, he kidnaps Dick Laurent, stuffs him in his trunk, and takes him into the desert. In the wasted sands he opens his trunk. The Mystery Man once more appears. He hands Fred a knife. Together, the two men kill Dick Laurent. Meanwhile, the police—policemen from Fred's story and Pete's narrative—investigate the murder of Andy. Inside Andy's house, these detectives claim that the main suspects are Fred Madison and Pete Dayton. In a photograph on the mantle appear Renee with Mr. Eddy and Alice with Andy. The film cuts back to Fred. He drives to his home. He rings the bell, waits for the intercom to click on, and then says, "Dick Laurent is dead." After uttering these words—the very first words of the film, by the way, which Fred hears on his intercom early one morning—Fred jumps in his car and drives off. The police are not far behind. The film ends by showing Fred driving down a dark highway with several police cars on his tail. Eventually, after many hours of this chase seem to have elapsed, he undergoes great pain, and his head appears to explode. The shot of the eerie highway again returns. The audience is left with a vision of a lonely road at night.

What is the meaning of these strange events? Clearly, Fred's two selves are beginning to blend and blur. He is no longer simply Fred, an egomaniac bent on controlling the real. He is no more solely Pete, an innocent who falls into sordid experience. He is somehow both at once, and thus an extremely confused man with no clear identity. Unable to live through his ego—this is Fred's problem—and unable to transcend his ego—this is the problem of Pete—this new amalgamation of Fred and Pete, Fred-Pete, is neither a self or an other, neither this person or that. He is but a ghostly creature, an attenuated presence doomed to inhabit a sort of limbo of half-existence. In this state, Fred-Pete loses all connection with reality. Once Renee leaves the hotel after making love with Dick Laurent, the real exits the film for good. Even though the earlier Fred and the earlier Pete could never grasp the real, at least they were on a quest for this entity. Now, Fred-Pete has given up on the quest and thus lives in a realm of unreality.

Fred arrives at the hotel where Renee and Dick Laurent make love. This mingling reveals the grafting of Fred onto Pete. Obviously, Fred did not murder Renee; he merely imagined her killing in a sick fantasy of total control of the real. Beyond any human control, Renee, the real, has of course eluded his violent tyranny. In the present case, Fred is no longer interested in connecting with the real. He simply lets Renee walk out of the hotel room and out of his life. He is now interested only in perceiving embodiments of his deepest fears. He focuses entirely on Dick Laurent, a manifestation of his jealous fear of never being loved. But in turning his attention to Laurent, he loses his sense of himself as Fred, however tenuous this sense is. Laurent is Pete's rival, not Fred's. In attacking Laurent, Fred to a certain extent becomes Pete. But this metamorphosis is not transcendence. On the contrary, it is confusion. Pete is not now a figure of transcendence; he is merely a replication of Fred, a man consumed by jealous fear. Turning Pete's rival into his own, Fred becomes a convoluted presence spread between two tortured selves. He turns into a sort of hermaphroditic being: neither one thing nor another but both at once. Thoroughly confused, he can only increase his confusion.

He falls into this increased confusion by killing part of himself. If this amalgamation of Fred and Pete had any wisdom, then this figure would understand that Laurent is a part of itself, a manifestation of its jealous fear. Unable to understand that this person is a projection of its inner turmoil, the Fred-Pete creature believes that murdering this person will serve as an act of cleansing revenge, a satisfying annihilation of an enemy. But this murdering of Laurent actually ensures that jealousy and fear will return with renewed fury into the bosom of Fred-Pete. At least Laurent's presence holds paranoia on the outside, where Fred-Pete can see it and possibly grasp it. With his presence terminated, the violent fear can only return firmly to the inside, where the mixture of Fred and Pete will no longer be able to see it.

That the Mystery Man helps the amalgamation of Fred and Pete to kill Laurent is apt. The dream of omniscience is ultimately a dream that the self and the world will be one, that no gap will exist between knower and known. In aiding Fred-Pete to reclaim its projection, the Mystery Man gives this figure the feeling that the cosmos is not outside but inside. But this feeling is of course misguided. Since the mixture of Fred and Pete is thoroughly confused and convoluted, then the world that it consumes will likewise be confused and convoluted. As yet another manifestation of Fred-Pete—an embodiment of its desire for controlling omniscience—the Mystery Man is a troubled guide, an unwitting siren song that leads his followers deeper into dangerous waters. Indeed, once he helps his follower kill Laurent, the Mystery Man disappears as well. He, too, becomes a projection recalled to its source, a presence digested and thus no longer visible.

These dangerous waters are not vigorous waves but the motionless surfaces of limbo. Having consumed egocentric paranoia, Dick Laurent, and having digested the hope for objective omniscience, the Mystery Man, the amalgamation of Pete and Fred has only one remaining outer concern—guilt, guilt over alleged violence toward others that is really violence toward self. This mixture of characters is masochistic in being sadistic, suicidal in being murderous. Left only with an awareness of guilt, this figure appropriately imagines in the end only policemen, policemen allegedly bent on capturing him for his killings of Andy and Laurent. After Fred-Pete announces to the former Fred that Dick Laurent is dead, this figure of amalgamation heads for the lost highway, where he will for all eternity, so it seems, flee from his potential captors. This is the most horrible of limbos, an endless flight from imagined pursuers, an existence that has no purpose but narcissistic paranoia, a feeling that everyone is "out to get me."

There appears to be no hope. Indeed, Fred Madison seems to have doomed himself to live forever in the same terrible round of experiences.[18] The film begins, recall, with Fred learning through his intercom that Dick Laurent is dead. At that point, he does not know that the message comes from his own voice. This version of Fred will of course end up killing Laurent and then announcing to an earlier version of Fred that Dick Laurent is dead. This circle is of course vicious, a repetition compulsion from which Fred will never escape. He will perpetually live the same tortured existence.

But one need not read the film as a failure of negative thinking at all. On the contrary, one can in all fairness interpret these final events as Fred's transcendence. In this alternate reading, Fred returns to finish the job that Pete began. Too innocent to sustain life's difficulties, Pete is unable to hold the negative vision for a long period of time. Learning from Pete's mistake, Fred comes back to solidify the power of the negative vision. In this regard, his last actions show him stripping away layers of selfhood and laying himself bare before the great and mysterious void. First of all, he leaves Renee alone. Instead of trying to impose his will upon her, he simply watches her and lets her go her way. He allows the real to be what it is. Secondly, he removes that part of himself that is paranoid and jealous. In killing Dick Laurent, he frees himself from violent tyranny; he releases his being into the flow of strange experience. Third, he escapes that other part of himself that desires total omniscience. After he kills Laurent, the Mystery Man disappears for good. Fourth, he reveals his awareness of his escape. In announcing Laurent's death in his intercom system, he is in essence telling himself that he has slain his paranoid side and is thus free to quest for reality as it is. Finally, he reaches union with the void. He escapes his pursuers—those parts of himself still connected to ego—and in the end sheds his body entirely. He becomes a spirit moving effortlessly over the empty highway, an invisible presence, one with the cosmos.

This alternate reading puts viewers in a difficult position. Now we are faced with two problems. The first has already been mentioned: we are never sure if we should take the events in the film as actual facts or psychological projections. The second problem is this: we are never certain if the film is about the failure of negative thinking or the success of this mode of exploration. Caught in both of these binds, we face hermeneutical emptiness, an inability ever to reach a definitive reading of the film.

The question then becomes: is this irreducible ambiguity mere confusion, or is it a form perfect for expressing the vision of negative theology? If we answer the former question in the affirmative, we are left in a state of simple befuddlement. However, if we answer yes to the latter question, then we discover ourselves stripped bare of any positive conclusions and thus extended into a realm of thorough negation, a place where no clear knowledge exists. Given Lynch's other cinematic forms, it is prudent to adhere to this position, to say that Lynch's structure is an apt vehicle for supporting a negative vision.

At the film's end, we indeed find ourselves floating over a lost highway, bewildered and troubled. But we know that this alienation from meaning, this divorce from significance, is the terrible preparation for an experience of the absolute, a gnosis of the divine. This is the terrible wisdom of Lynch's *Lost Highway*.

NOTES

1. Chris Rodley, ed., *Lynch on Lynch*, rev. ed. (New York: Faber & Faber, 2005), 222.

2. The film seems to teach this lesson negatively. Indeed, the movie appears to be about a man who cannot give up his desire to control the world through his rational conceptions. As Martha P. Nochimson argues, "Fred is doomed by his relationship to Renee not because of *her* inconsistencies but because of *his* obsessions. Through Fred's tenacity concerning Renee, instead of portraying the rewards of the will to lose one's will Lynch portrays the catastrophe of being unable to do so" (*The Passion of David Lynch: Wild at Heart in Hollywood* (Austin: University of Texas Press, 1997), 209).

3. Deirdre Carabine, *The Unknown God: Negative Theology in the Platonic Tradition, Plato to Eriugena* (Louvain, Belgium: Peeters Press, 1995), 85.

4. Ibid., 135–38.

5. Ibid., 279–93.

6. Here I'm following Nochimson (*Passion of David Lynch*, 209–16).

7. Eric Bryant Rhodes notes that Lynch himself called the film a "psychogenic fugue." This term refers to a "mental state in which a person is delusional although seemingly fully aware, a state from which he emerges with no memory of his actions" ("Review of *Lost Highway*," *Film Quarterly* 51, no. 3 (Spring 1998): 59). If Fred suffers from this disorder—and Rhodes thinks he does—then the film is "Fred's hallucination" (ibid.). From another angle, Tom O'Connor argues that "Fred desires that the actual world around him reflect his own idealized position above it" ("The Pitfalls of Media 'Rep-

resentations': David Lynch's *Lost Highway*," *The Journal of Film and Video* 57, no. 3 [Fall 2005]: 15). Hence, he can't tell the difference between "representation" and "reality" (ibid.). The film itself, O'Connor continues, likewise features this blurring between representation and real—audiences never know if they are witnessing actual occurrences or Fred's hallucinations. This blurring results in what N. Katherine Hayles and Nicholas Gessler term "the slipstream of mixed reality" (quoted in O'Connor, 15). Marina Warner adds to this sense: *Lost Highway*, she claims, "is all illusion, almost buoyantly ironic, for you can enter the story at any point and the straight road you're traveling down will unaccountably turn back on itself and bring you back to where you started" ("Voodoo Road: David Lynch's New Identity-swap Chiller *Lost Highway* Reflects the Fractured Image of the Modern Narcissus," *Sight and Sound* 7, no. 8 [1997]: 6).

8. Bernd Herzogenrath in his Lacanian reading indeed argues that the film "negates the idea of the autonomous, stable individual" ("On the *Lost Highway*: Lynch and Lacan, Cinema and Cultural Pathology," *Other Voices* 1, no. 3 [January 1999]: 2, www/othervoices.org/1.3/bh/ highway.html). He claims that Fred suffers from something akin to multiple personality disorder. He is a "split, decentered subject" (ibid., 16).

9. I borrow this term from Victoria Nelson. She uses it to describe literature in which "inner psychic processes are projected sympathetically onto an exterior landscape" (*The Secret Life of Puppets* [Cambridge, MA: Harvard University Press, 2002], 110–11).

10. Slavoj Žižek takes issue with this reading of the film, maintaining that this "Jungian" notion of psychic projection ties itself into a "New Age reading" of the film that focuses "on the flow of subconscious Life Energy that allegedly connects all events and runs through all scenes and persons, turning Lynch into the poet of a Jungian universal subconscious spiritualized Libido" (*The Art of the Ridiculous Sublime: On David Lynch's* Lost Highway [Seattle: University of Washington Press, 2000], 3). (Žižek picks out Nochimson as the prime exponent of this reading.) In contrast, Žižek reads the film through the lens of Lacan to argue that Lynch's films, especially Lost Highway, explore the ways in which fantasies making up "reality" protect us from the "Real"—the unspeakably sublime energy that is excessively enjoyable and horrific. For Žižek, the film is ultimately about how Fred constructs fantasies to save him from having to face the sublimity of the real. My main argument in this book basically falls between Nochimson's and Žižek's. Like Nochimson, I believe that Lynch's films are hopeful explorations of the redemptive powers of rejecting the controlling concepts of the rational will. Like Žižek, I maintain that the powers beyond the fantasies of reason (or desire) are unrepresentable, sublime. Indeed, like Žižek—but in the terminology of Romanticism—I believe that all representations of reality are ironic fantasies both defending against while opening to the powers of the Real—in my case, the holy, the sublime power of Being. In sum, in my mind

Žižek picks up on epistemological complexities that Nochimson tends to overlook.

11. Herzogenrath reaches a similar conclusion: "the film ironically personifies Fred's timeless desire to be general over representation itself in the Mystery Man" ("On the *Lost Highway,*" 6).

12. Anne Jerslev argues that the film is indeed about "an imaginary journey into the very essence of jealousy," an "ecstatic nightmarish vision about woman as fatal mystery and uncontrollable desire" ("Beyond Boundaries: David Lynch's *Lost Highway,*" in *The Cinema of David Lynch: American Dreams, Nightmare Visions,* ed. Erica Sheen and Annette Davison, 151–64 [New York: Wallflower Press, 2005], 156). In this nightmare, Renee/Alice remains a "mystery" (ibid., 155).

13. In his Lacanian reading of the film, Todd McGowan argues that Fred is consumed with desire and thus dwells in reality while Pete enjoys desire fulfilled and there lives in fantasy. Or, in McGowan's words: "fantasy serves as a respite from the ambiguity of desire" ("Finding Ourselves on a 'Lost Highway': David Lynch's Lesson in Fantasy," *Cinema Journal* 39, no. 2 [2000]: 51). McGowan claims that most films merge desire and fantasy, making them almost indistinguishable. *Lost Highway,* in contrast, divides these two modes.

14. Martin Heidegger claims that negative theology is akin to stepping back from philosophical traditions that set up positive concepts through which to perceive and name being (*On Time and Being,* trans. Joan Stambaugh (New York: Harper & Row, 1972), 47).

15. In this way, he's like Nochimson's version of Frank in *Passion of David Lynch.*

16. This transitional space is akin to the "red room" in *Twin Peaks,* Dorothy's apartment in *Blue Velvet,* and the radiator in *Eraserhead.*

17. According to Nochimson, Fred never moves beyond the "toxic, lower elements of the subconscious." In this way, he is little different from Frank (*Passion of David Lynch,* 213). It is indeed true that Fred on one level seems unable to make the transformation successfully undertaken by Jeffrey and Sailor.

18. Lynch famously called the film a "Möbius strip." For Warner, this metaphor is apt, for in the film, she argues, Lynch bends the arrow of time into an endless and twisted circle ("Voodoo Road: David Lynch's New Identity-swap Chiller *Lost Highway* Reflects the Fractured Image of the Modern Narcissus," *Sight and Sound* 7, no. 8 (1997): 6). According to Greg Hainge, "the establishment of this loop . . . actually allows that very loop to be exceeded and . . . consequently signals the complete dissolution of narrative . . . logic and linear time" ("Weird or Loopy? Specular Spaces, Feedback, and Artifice in *Lost Highway's* Aesthetics of Sensation, " in *The Cinema of David Lynch: American Dreams, Nightmare Visions,* ed. Erica Sheen and Annette Davison, 136–50 [New York: Wallflower Press, 2005], 145).

CHAPTER FIVE

Real Dreams in *Mulholland Dr.*

The Dream Detective

In an interview conducted near the release of *Mulholland Dr.*, Lynch offered a clue for understanding his most enigmatic of movies. Lynch was asked if he at times enjoyed "teasing or mystifying the viewer." After responding "no," Lynch claimed that the confusing parts of this film and of all his films emerge from the "idea." This idea, he claimed, simply comes to a creator unannounced. The creator is then beholden to shape the idea the way that the idea wants to be shaped. The creator, Lynch continued, must at all costs be "true" to this idea, whatever it may be. Though the idea might be irreducibly strange, it still contains "clues" to its meaning. The "clues," Lynch concluded, are among the most beautiful parts of a riddling film. They are beautiful because all of us are "detectives." "We mull things over," Lynch stated, "and we figure things out. We're always working in this way. People's minds hold things and form conclusions with indications." Lynch likened this hermeneutical activity to the way people understand music. After the music starts, a theme suggests itself. This theme disappears, but when it again returns, "it's so much greater than what's gone before." Near the end of this sequence of the interview, Lynch concluded that the viewers of *Mulholland Dr.* must play detective, that they must enter into the film as a detective would a mystery, as a music lover would a bizarre fugue[1]—as, one might add, a dreamer would a curious dream.

One might add the last comparison for obvious reasons: *Mulholland Dr.* is replete with dreams. Indeed, the entire film might be a dream. While inside a dream—whether it be one's own dream or another's—one must necessarily be a detective, a solver of mysteries, an inquiring presence endlessly attempting to piece together the outlandish fragments of the overcharged unconscious. Obviously, one must become a detective when analyzing a dream after the fact. Like a Jung or a Freud—or even like an Ezekiel or a St. John—one must try to discover latent content in the midst of strange events. But one must also be a detective from *within* the dream. In the midst of the dream sequence, some interpretive presence must remain, a being, however tenuous and ghostly, that negotiates among the symbols and the gists, the hints and the clues, and tries diligently to understand the meanings, to get at the essence of most any dream: the quest for identity. To parse a dream vision from within the dream is to struggle to understand in a preliminary way what the dream has to tell about the self, about the self and the world. This is precisely Diane Selwyn's great problem. This protagonist (Naomi Watts) of *Mulholland Dr.* must from within her own dream discover who she is and what her purpose is.[2] She must as a detective of dream shape the clues into a somewhat cogent narrative whose meaning is fatal for her deepest being. Undertaking this task—as mysterious as the dream itself—she is to her dream as we are to Lynch's film: in the midst of mysterious ideas, hoping to find what lies beneath the gorgeous surfaces and unforgettable sheens.

In exploring the role of the dreamer in the dream insofar as this role relates to identity, *Mulholland Dr.* inflects a long religious tradition: the transformative dream vision. This tradition begins with the biblical visions of Ezekiel and Daniel, but it thrives most mightily in the Middle Ages, in the literary dream visions of Chaucer and the Pearl poet. These dream visions suggest that the dreamer is a detective within his dream, a presence attempting to understand his relationship to the divine, to his sacred identity. Unable to grasp this identity in the waking world, the dreamer requires the unworldly landscape and logic of dream in order to explore the essential recesses of self. In this interior space, one can see and say things that the noontime consciousness will not allow. There in the lonely chambers of dream, one is able to envision curious possibilities and to explore untoward potentials. There in Morpheus's urgent corridors, one can perhaps witness a wholeness unavailable in the fragmented world of waking, a ravishing ideal. If one can behold this harmony, then one might secure a model on which to base his waking consciousness, a standard of behavior toward which to quest under the aching sun.

Lynch's *Mulholland Dr.* inflects precisely this sort of dream: a dream of an ideal realm inaccessible in the hopelessly botched waking world. Drawing generally from this sort of dream vision, Lynch's film reflects a particular sort of medieval dream vision: the prophetic dream, the window to eternity. These dreams typically featured a mentor figure explaining to the dreamer the mysteries of the heavenly realm. Such dreams were at once apocalyptic and skeptical. They were apocalyptic because they revealed unworldly harmonies unseen in the mundane regions. They were skeptical because they were suspicious of the empirical world. Such was the "Gnostic" flavor of the medieval dream vision. Regardless of its Christian emphasis, it was hungry for a supernatural realm beyond the precincts of ruined nature.

Emphasizing these two primary qualities of the dream vision—its apocalyptic vigor and its skeptical rigor—*Mulholland Dr.* shares with Lynch's earlier pictures a yen for spiritual transcendence and a suspicion toward worldly ideology. Like all of Lynch's religious films, *Mulholland Dr.* questions the validity of the status quo. The film appears to say this: the realm of space and time that most take seriously is hopelessly ruined, a place of fragmentation and fear, of deceit and of death. In the face of this wreck of the world, all one can hope for is the solace of the unreal, of dream. This dream might be mere escapism, but it also could constitute a suitable ideal toward which one might strive in the midst of fallen nature. If this latter possibility is valid, then the dream vision, regardless of its unworldliness, might still give the tortured cosmos some meaning, some purpose. Exploring this potential of the dream vision, *Mulholland Dr.* suggests a troubling reversal: everyday, empirical reality is meaningless; extraordinary, invisible dream is significant. This reversal is virtually nihilistic. It suggests Lynch's cinematic vision has become increasingly skeptical toward the redemptive possibilities of this world.

In *Mulholland Dr.*, the protagonist Diane Selwyn appears to be wrecked by her temporal existence. (I say "appears," because Lynch blurs the distinction between fantasy and fact; for this reason, I stick to the subjunctive through this paragraph.) After ostensibly winning a jitterbug contest in Canada and coming to Los Angeles, Diane seemingly suffers serious heartbreak. In this state, she undergoes a dream vision of wholeness. In this lengthy dream—it constitutes the first two-thirds of the film—Diane pictures herself as Betty Elm (also Naomi Watts), an ingénue actress recently arrived in Los Angeles. There she soon meets a woman named Rita (Laura Elena Harring). When Betty learns that Rita suffers amnesia, the young actress turns detective and undertakes to help her friend find out who she really is. In doing so, she is also on a quest to find out who she herself is. While Betty and Rita— two halves of one self, it seems—are undertaking their journeys toward wholeness, we learn that a Hollywood conspiracy controls the movie industry. This hidden corps of controllers is apparently hunting Rita; they are also seemingly the reason why Betty never gets her big break. Depicting the quest for identity and the forces that try to quell this quest, Diane's dream is both apocalyptic and skeptical. It is apocalyptic in its revelation of the mysteries of wholeness. It is skeptical in its suspicion toward the institutions of the waking world. At once revelatory of the archetype and dubious towards time, Diane's dream suggests that in dreams only do we find solace and possibly truth.

The film is organized to make dream look like reality and reality look like dream. After a bizarre opening that shows a dreamy jitterbug sequence, the film turns to what appears to be a "realist" narrative—a world of sharp texture and cogent narrative. This narrative features Betty and Rita questing for identity and challenging the secret controllers. The story seems to be the movie proper. But after an hour or so, the movie changes radically. Following an outlandish scene at Club Silencio, a woman wakes up. She is Diane Selwyn. Though she resembles Betty (indeed, Betty and Diane are both played by the same actress), she is depressed and drab where Betty is exuberant and bright. Diane's narrative, seemingly real, feels like a dream: it is fragmented, surreal, and unpredictable. Her reality appears to be unreal, while her dream life is ostensibly reality.[3] Why does Lynch push for this reversal?

Lynch seems to for a very good reason: he again wants his cinematic form to support his filmic content. The dream vision, as we have seen, calls for a disturbing reversal of expectations. We normally connect truth with waking consciousness and illusion with the images of dream. The dream vision turns this expectation on its head, asking us to link dream with ultimate truth and to associate waking consciousness with delusional perception. Such an upending blurs the time-honored distinction between dream and reality. In the wake of such a reversal, we are confused. What we thought was reality might well be a dream, and what we earlier considered dream could now be reality. If reality is a dream and dream is reality, then how do we know if we're awake or asleep? How can we tell if we're walking on solid ground or floating in air? How can we discern between solid perception and hallucination?

In formally casting his film as a dream vision, Lynch makes viewers feel in their bones the strange ironies of dream. They must ask the startling questions of all dream visionaries. Is the waking world worthwhile, or is it fallen beyond repair? Is the dreaming realm truthful, or is it a mere flight from everyday responsibility? These inquiries concerning the potential apocalypse of the dream and the possible unreality of the empirical necessarily turn audiences into spiritual seekers, into men and women keen on scouring the interior spaces for cosmic truth and on doubting the solidity of exteriors.

The Dream Vision

The Western dream vision reaches back to biblical and classical sources. We recall the apocalyptic dream visions of Ezekiel, who witnessed God's glory by the river Chobar, and of St. John of Patmos, who saw the end of the world from his cave. We remember the equally revelatory visions of Plato as he meditated on Er and of Macrobius as he commented on Scipio. In each case, the dream is an intermediary between the sacred world and the profane one.

The dreamer appears in the dream as a recipient of divine vision. From this vision, he gains a truth unavailable in the waking world.

European poets during the Middle Ages drew on these scattered instances of apocalyptic dream to establish a new genre of poetry: the dream vision. Though based on the biblical and classical sources listed above, this genre—employed by Guillaume de Lorris, Jean de Muen, Geoffrey Chaucer, and the Pearl poet—found its systematic form mainly in Macrobius's commentary on Cicero's conclusion to *De Re Publica*, a description of an apocalyptic dream of Scipio. In his commentary, Macrobius distinguishes five different types of dream. The first type is the *insomnium*, the nightmare, never to be taken seriously. The next kind is the *visium*, or the hallucination, also not to be taken seriously. The third type of dream and all those thereafter are serious forms, possible bearers of truths unavailable in the waking world. The *somnium*, the enigmatic dream, is robustly ambiguous, replete with outlandish shapes and obscuring veils. It requires detailed interpretation. Often the *somnium* takes the form of the *oraculum*, or the prophetic dream in which a mentor leads the dreamer through the intricacies of the dream landscape. Usually, this parental figure unveils to the dreamer a hidden destiny and the appropriate advice for following or avoiding this destiny. The last kind of dream, the *visio*, also frequently takes the enigmatic form of the *somnium*. This visionary dream is a prophecy that presents itself directly to the dreamer, without the mediation of a kind mentor. It frequently reveals the nature of the afterlife and thus the true and sacred identity of the dreamer.[4]

Understandably, epistemological difficulties abound, mainly in two forms. As Macrobius notes, almost all dreams, regardless of type, are hopelessly enigmatic and thus require extensive interpretation. This interpretation, however, is just as likely to be wrong as it is right—the meanings of dreams are indeed probably beyond the scope of human wisdom. Another problem, as Macrobius makes clear, is this: the types of dream generally overlap. When dealing with a synthesis of the last three types of dream, this is not a terrible problem. Even if a dream combines elements of the *somnium*, the *oraculum*, and the *visio*, the dream is at least ostensibly on prophetic ground and therefore likely to possess real authority.

But what if this *somnium* or the *oraculum* or the *visio*—or all three combined—contains traces of the nightmare or the hallucination? How is one to know if the dream can be trusted? Might it be sent from a demon hoping to seduce the dreamer into destructive sin? Might it be entirely unreal?[5]

Of course the deeper problem behind these two difficulties is this: one can never be entirely sure concerning the authority of dreams. Dreams as truths and dreams as illusions often look the very same, so one can never be sure if one is getting fact or fantasy. This awful problem is compounded by a related one, even more onerous: if the dream is a bearer of truth—if it possesses real authority—then it reveals waking reality to be a sham, a realm unable to reach higher truths. This reversal—dream is reality and reality is dream—results in an epistemological crisis: the inability to tell the difference between dream and reality, sleeping and waking. A related problem occurs if the dream is merely an illusion, if it possesses no authority. If this is the case, then promising dreams are mere ghosts and fragmented reality is all we have. This situation—healing visions are false and empirical limitation is true—can quickly lead to despair.

The Dream Factory

Mulholland Dr. opens with a dreamlike sequence. Several high school kids dance the jitterbug against a muted purple background. Their images fade in and out of one another. Eventually, a beautiful young blonde-haired woman dominates the screen. She is bathed in light to the point of being luminously white. An old man (Dan Birbaum) and an old woman (Jeanne Bates) stand on either side of her. Applause surrounds her. She appears to have won a prize, probably the prize for winning the jitterbug contest.

The camera then apparently takes the point of view of someone lowering her head to wrinkled red sheets. The light on this image is much duller and the contours are much sharper than in the earlier sequence. We appear now to be away from the world of teenybopper dreams of jitterbug contests. We wonder if the reclining head is moving toward sleep or even death. We are ostensibly now in a "real" world, sordid and bland.

The next scenes take place as the opening credits roll. These scenes are vividly "realistic." A long black limousine cruises over a dark highway. It stops. Two large men in the driver's and the passenger's seats turn to face a gorgeous woman with black hair in an evening dress. One man points a gun at her. It is time for her to die. A car filled with joy-riding kids slams into the limousine. Everyone is apparently killed but the woman with black hair. Stumbling, confused, and bleeding from the head, she makes her way from the road—Mulholland Dr.—down to the city below—Los Angeles. After crossing Sunset Boulevard, she sleeps under some bushes. In the morning, she sneaks into an apartment vacated by an actress (Maya Bond) going away to a film shoot. She hides in a cabinet and again goes to sleep.

The film then switches to a diner. A troubled man (Patrick Fischler) tells another (Michael Cooke) about a nightmare he had. The dream actually features the first man in the diner with the second. In the dream, after the two eat and the second man pays, the two men walk behind the diner. As the two men round the corner at the back of the building, a hideous creature appears. This creature embodies pure evil. It horrifies the dreamer. After the first man finishes his tale of the dream, he and the second man walk to the back of the diner as if to prove that the dream could not be reality. But as the two men round the corner at the back of the building, a terrifying man appears as though from nowhere. The man who had the dream is so terrified that his heart stops. He ostensibly dies on the spot.

After the camera switches back to the black-haired woman sleeping inside a cabinet, it then moves to a large man with a small head sitting in a strange chair in the middle of a dimly lighted room. He (Michael J. Anderson) wears a headset with a mouthpiece attached. In his ear a dial tone sounds, followed by the ringing of the phone. The film switches to the back of another man's head. He seems to sit at the front desk of a large, ornate hotel. He answers the phone. The camera returns to the man with the small head. He says into his mouthpiece: "The girl is still missing." The camera comes back to the man in the hotel. He dials a number. A dirty yellow phone rings. A hand picks up the phone and a voice says, "Talk to me." This hand then presses down the receiver and dials another number. A phone resting under a lurid red lamp and beside a dirty ashtray rings.

The camera then moves to an airport. The beautiful young blonde woman whom we earlier saw bathed in light appears. She is exiting the airport with the kind old woman who earlier stood beside her. This young woman, named, we find, Betty, makes it clear that she has just arrived in Los Angeles in hopes of becoming a Hollywood star. An old man walks out of the airport. He also stood with the young woman earlier. He is apparently the older woman's husband. As Betty talks amiably with the old couple, she loses track of her luggage. Just when she thinks it's been stolen, she realizes that a cabbie has kindly loaded it into his trunk. She happily gets into the cab. The older couple then appear in the back of a moving limousine. They look at each other and laugh maniacally. It seems as though they are in on some inside joke.

Betty arrives at the apartment where the woman with the black hair was sleeping within the cabinet. As we learn from a conversation from the apartment's supervisor (Ann Miller), Betty is the niece of the actress who has vacated the apartment. Betty is going to stay in the apartment while she tries to break into the movie business. When Betty enters the apartment, she is surprised to find a dark-haired woman taking a shower. The two share an awkward greeting. Betty assumes that the woman is a friend of her aunt's. When Betty asks the woman's name, the woman doesn't respond. She seems unable to remember. After Betty leaves the woman to finish her shower, the woman notices in the bathroom a poster advertising *Gilda*, a Rita Hayworth picture. When she emerges from the bathroom wearing only a towel, she tells Betty that her name is Rita. Betty then notices that Rita has sustained a wound to the head. When Betty offers to help, Rita simply says that she needs to sleep more. She then lies down on the bed and immediately slumbers.

So begins *Mulholland Dr.* What are we to make of this quick succession of sequences? The opening jitterbug sequence appears to be something out of a strange dream. Against an artificial purple background, energetic dancers blend and blur. From this welter emerges a woman bathed in unnatural white light. What follows, it seems, is not a dream at all, but real. Compared to the jitterbug sequence, the red sheets toward which the head declines seem to be palpable, empirically solid. The events that follow seem realistic as well, composed as they are of vivid sequences linked together through imagery and linear narrative. However, these events are also replete with people sleeping, talk of dreams, and Hollywood movie imagery. Soon after the car crash, the woman later known as Rita falls asleep under bushes. Is what follows her dream? Rita then goes into slumber in a cabinet. Does she dream here as well? Would what follows be a dream within a dream? Rita later goes to sleep again. Are the events that come after another dream? Would these occurrences then be part of a dream within a dream within a dream? In the midst of this potentially infinite regression of dreaming, a man recounts a dream that then comes true. Does this tell us that dreams are the bearers of reality and that reality can easily turn into a dream? If so, then how can we tell the difference between what is actually lived and what is dreamed? These possible dreams and this discourse on dream take place in the province of the dream factory, in Hollywood. Rita's traffic accident occurs on Mulholland Dr., a road hovering above Hollywood, acting, as it were, as a boundary between the movie world and the non-movie world. As she stumbles into the city, she crosses Sunset Boulevard, famous not only for the Hollywood film based on its name but also for its associations with the old stars of Hollywood. Once installed in the apartment, she takes on the identity of a dead Hollywood starlet. These Hollywood connections suggest that we are in a world of artifice, of dreams, of false identities.[6]

Truth and Dream

If we are in a world where the difference between dream and reality, sleeping and waking, collapses, then we are compelled to ask this question: are all dreams created equally? In other words, are some dreams more "true" than others; that is, are some dreams eminently rich, powerful, whole, and thus capable of enlightening the dreamer, of showing her an ideal identity, a sacred vision of who she should most be? After our discussion of medieval dream visions, we certainly know that some dreams are superior to others, that some bear truth while others are mere hallucinations. Against this background, Nietzsche and Jung offer instructive modern recapitulations of medieval dream theory. Both theorists suggest that some dreams are more likely to capture the sacred power of life. These special dreams, Nietzsche and Jung suggest, are not meaningless mysteries or full solutions. On the contrary, they are strange syntheses of the silence at the heart of life and the noise by which we try to express this curious core.

Nietzsche in his work on the inauguration of tragedy memorably claims that the cosmos is composed of two great principles: the Dionysian abyss—the realm of silent, inhuman, and indifferent physical reality—and the Apollonian illusion—the plane of meaningful, humanized, differentiated art. The former part of existence is horrifying, a great gulf of insignificance and death, but it is also exhilarating, a level of existence where all is one, a sign of the ungraspable surge of life. The latter component of existence is false, an unrealistic dream of full meaning and persistent order. But this element is often at the same time essential, a vision of elegant and ideal organization, a witness to human purpose and identity.[7] I say that the Apollonian is "often" essential because not all illusions of enduring order are created equally. As Nietzsche suggests, most works of art are either too turbulent, and thus bordering on Dionysian insignificance, or too decorous, and therefore utterly divorced from Dionysian energy. However, some works of art, like, say, Attic tragedy, perfectly blend turbulence and pattern, abysmal profundity and pleasing harmony.[8] These works of art are whole, integrated, impossible marriages of opposites: chaos and order, emptiness and form, will and idea, truth and illusion. These works achieve the concord of Jung's fully realized self, a dynamic blending of the collective unconscious—an undifferentiated abyss, a plenitude beyond human reasoning—and the conscious ego—a distinct form, a pattern of human knowing. For Jung, the collective, though ineffable, is the enduring source of life, and the individual, though meaningful, is a temporary form of existence.[9] In sum, for both Nietzsche and Jung, some dreams are capable of organizing and partially revealing the abyss. These dreams resemble waves on the ocean, eddies in the river; they are tense and tenuous and torqued forms of bewildering depths and lubricious energies, of silences always just beyond speech, of the nothing generating all things.

The early scenes in *Mulholland Dr.* give us no real clue as to who is dreaming the various dreams. This is probably an unimportant detail. What does seem to be important, however, is the nature of the dreams. Are they so turbulent as to be meaningless; or are they so ordered as to be vapid? Or are these dreams in fact profound marriages between intractable mystery and cogent solution, ineffable void and luminous form? If the dreams do prove to be syntheses between these poles, then we can conclude that these dreams are somehow "true," visions of wholeness. For whom, if anyone, they are visions of wholeness can only be revealed later. At this later date, it will seem that these dreams are the issue of the troubled soul of Diane Selwyn, though we can never be sure.

The dreams, regardless of who is dreaming them, are focused on the question of identity, namely the identities of two women—Betty and Rita. If we can take the dreams together, as if they compose one larger dream—the dream that is the film itself—then we can conclude that Betty and Rita are two halves of one self, each of which is in search of a principle of completion, a sacred other that will result in a harmonious whole. This conclusion is one of the few that is clearly suggested by the film.[10]

Let us, for instance, take the character of Betty. She arrives in Hollywood in search of a new identity, an identity as a Hollywood star. From the minute she lands in movieland, she finds herself caught up in a mystery, the mystery of whether she has within her the stuff of stardom, the energy to become an ideal icon, a model of perfection that others will follow. She spends her time in the film questing for this ideal identity; like a detective, she interprets the clues around her in hopes of discovering her mysterious center. Let us then turn to Rita's character. After suffering amnesia from a car crash, she must also try to find out who she is. From the instant that she emerges from the crash, she too finds herself caught in a mystery, the mystery of what her history is and what her destiny is going to be. She is likewise a detective in the film, someone in search of clues that will ultimately help her discover her enduring self.[11]

But these quests are in the end inseparable. Betty immediately becomes involved in Rita's quest to find out who she really is. In fact, she instigates and organizes the investigation. After Rita sits on a bed crying and lamenting that she doesn't know who she is, Betty decides to help this vulnerable woman at all costs. All the clues they have to go on are three. Rita has in her possession a black leather handbag containing thousands of dollars and a strangely shaped blue key. Rita is injured in the head and recalls Mulholland Dr., as though she has suffered a car crash. Rita believes that the name Diane Selwyn is significant. Based on these scant clues, Betty first suggests that she and Rita find out if an accident did indeed occur on Mulholland Dr. the night before. On the phone to the police, Betty mimics a concerned citizen and finds out that an accident did occur. Betty then resolves to track down Diane. Soon after her first audition at Paramount, Betty accompanies Rita to the apartment complex where Diane apparently lives. When the two women eventually find Diane's apartment, they knock on the door. When there is no answer, Betty climbs in through a window. Once she enters the apartment, she is beset by an awful odor. After she lets Rita in, the two wander into the bedroom. There they find a woman, ostensibly Diane, dead. She has been shot in the head. The two women rush back to Betty's aunt's apartment. There, Rita decides to disguise herself. She fears that she is involved in something terrible and criminal— that she is either a murderer or about to be murdered. Betty again takes the initiative. She cuts off Rita's long black hair and chooses for her a blonde wig that falls almost to the shoulders. Now, Betty and Rita share the same hair color and style. One wonders if Rita's new "blonde" identity—this resemblance to Betty, her plucky guide—is really the self for which Rita has been questing. Immediately after she takes on Betty's appearance, the two women express their affection for one another by making passionate love. This steamy scene is more intense and "real" than anything Rita has done heretofore. It seems as though she has "found herself" in the arms of Betty, regardless of her forgotten history.

The same might be said of Betty. Ostensibly, she discovers her true identity in the arms of her guide, Rita. Upon first entering Los Angeles, Betty is a wide-eyed ingénue, unable even to look after her own luggage. When she finds a dark and mysterious and beautiful woman in her aunt's apartment, she quickly moves from innocence to experience. In deciding to help this distressed woman, she becomes, in a sense, another version of Lynch's Jeffrey Beaumont. She proves that she's willing to break the laws of decorum in order to find "knowledge" and "experience." She first of all harbors the strange Rita against the advice of her aunt and also protects her against the prying and suspicious supervisor of the apartment complex. She next lies to the police—impersonating a concerned citizen—in order to gather information concerning the accident. Then, during her audition at Paramount, she interprets her scene in the sultriest and sexiest way possible, turning a clichéd melodramatic scene into an erotic masterpiece. She follows this transgressive scene by breaking into and entering the apartment of a total stranger. Next she aids and abets someone who might be a fugitive from the law. Finally, she instigates and engages in lesbian sex, surely an outré act for someone "fresh from the farm" like Betty. During this act, Betty realizes that she is in love with Rita, her double. Realizing this, she appears to find out who she really is—what she loves, what she likes to do. Like Rita, she "finds herself" in the arms of her guide, discovers her sacred and enduring identity in the passion of a dream.

During their lovemaking session, the two women become one. Each has completed the other. Each resembles the other. Each penetrates the other. This merging of separate creatures into one identity suggests that Betty and Diane are really two halves of one fully integrated, harmonious self. Betty's overly cute spunkiness is delimited and complemented by Rita's sultry reserve. Rita's dangerously distressed passivity is curbed and completed by Betty's optimistic activity. One could put this complementary relationship in other terms as well. Betty is the industrious consciousness; Rita is the mysterious unconscious. Betty is reason; Rita is emotion. Betty is light; Rita is dark. Betty is the "man"; Rita is the "woman." Whatever the opposition, Betty and Rita reconcile the poles. Theirs is the perfect synthesis, the sacred marriage.

With this realization of self—in which separate entities find their complements and thus merge into a great whole—comes knowledge, a gnosis into the relationship between dream and reality, manifestation and abyss. Soon after Betty and Rita fall into a post-sex slumber, Rita starts to talk in her sleep. She says "No

Hay Banda" and repeats "Silencio" again and again. That she reveals such a clue in her sleep suggests that the unconscious has broken through consciousness, that a message from the mysterious beyond has made its way to the rational present. Betty and Rita soon understand that this word refers to a nightclub. With Rita wearing her wig—and thus looking like Betty—the women make their way to this club in the middle of the night. It is located in a deserted and windy part of the city, almost as if it's some place out of time. (In this sense, it recalls the desert house of the "fence" in *Lost Highway*, a transitional place between fact and fantasy, reality and dream, eternity and time.) Betty and Rita enter this "Club Silencio"—which itself could be a part of yet another dream, the collective dream of the sleeping and now unified Betty and Rita. On this borderline between silence and noise, emptiness and form, they understand the relationship between illusion and truth, recording and original.

A master of ceremonies (Richard Green) appears on a dimly lighted stage. He wears a red suit and sports a devilish goatee. He immediately establishes the theme of his strange speech: speaking sometimes in Spanish and other times in English, he states that everything is a recording. He calls for a trumpet player. One (Conte Candoli) appears and seems to play his trumpet. However, the MC quickly reports that the player is merely mimicking a recorded trumpet. His point is clear. Everything that we see and hear is a copy of an absent original. All is, in this way, derivative, artificial—a film. Life is an immense movie whose script and director have disappeared. It is an illusion divorced from truth, a dream.

This first MC steps aside. A second one (Geno Silva) appears. He wears a bright yellow suit. He is the same man who earlier appeared as "Cookie," the owner of a seedy hotel. This repetition of the same character suggests that characters from so-called "real" life are really just recordings, imitations, actors, figures from dreams. This yellow MC then introduces Rebekeh Del Rio. A woman emerges from behind the stage curtain. She really is Rebekeh Del Rio, the famous singer. She plays herself, intimating, again, that we are all playing a role separate from an authentic self. Ms. Del Rio walks to the microphone. The camera focuses in on her heavily made up face. She seemingly begins to sing a version of

Roy Orbison's "Crying" in Spanish. Halfway through this moving and beautiful number, she collapses. However, the song continues to play on. It is clearly a recording. Ms. Del Rio has been lip-synching a song recorded from her very own voice. This song is a translation of the English original. She imitates an imitation of an imitation. This vertiginous situation hints at an infinite regress. We are all imitations of imitations of imitations. How can we ever access the real? What is ultimately behind imitations? Are all imitations equal? Are some forms closer to the mystery than others?

The reaction of Betty and Rita partially answers these questions. While Ms. Del Rio appears to sing her song, the two women cry uncontrollably. They are obviously deeply moved by Ms. Del Rio's full-hearted version of Orbison's plaintive song. This enthusiastically melancholy response suggests this: some imitations are more profound than others; some copies actually capture something akin to authenticity—to the depth of life, the mystery of existence. This depth and this mystery might remain forever inaccessible. Still, their expanse and their weirdness appear in certain works of art, certain illusions that capture the turbulence of wild and tragic emotions. This turbulence is akin to the abysmal energy behind all discrete forms, to the Dionysian indifference underlying all Apollonian distinction, to the unconscious gulf underneath the conscious ego. Put another way, this organized chaos of artful pathos details the relationship between ungraspable silence and accessible song, between Club Silencio and the Spanish "Crying." This relationship reveals all that we can ever know of reality: the graspable world is a dream, a distorted copy of an inaccessible and silent original; however, some dreams are capable of unveiling the ineffable nature of this abysmal original. These dreams are what we call art, great art, the kind that moves our souls to strange, spontaneous tears or to uncanny eruptions of laughter or to stunned, unmoored silences. If there is such a thing as "reality," it can only be grasped through profound dreams. If life is only "dream," then some dreams can reveal mysterious reality.[12]

This is the gnosis reached by Betty and Rita, the harmonious and whole self. This self, this marriage of opposites (of pattern and turbulence, consciousness and the unconscious) apprehends the nature of existence, its real dreams and its dreamed reality. Realizing this interplay between silence and song, abyss and art, Betty and Rita weep in the face of the profundity. Moreover, this same self discovers the solution to a mystery that has hounded it from early on—it finds the lock to the blue key. While she weeps, Betty, one side of the self, the rational side, reaches into her purse. There she sees a blue box. She understands. This is the destination of the key. She summons Rita. The two of them return to the apartment and take down the black handbag. They place the key into the blue box. Betty disappears. Then Rita vanishes. The aunt walks through the apartment, looking for the source of a strange sound she has heard. The blue box disappears. It was all a dream. Betty and Rita, it seems, never existed.

But of course they did. They existed in the dream—in the recording of reality, in the film. They enjoy, seemingly, the same "ontological" status of everything else. But, in fact, Betty and Rita enjoy *more* ontological status than most dream images. Like Ms. Del Rio's song—like Lynch's film—they participate in a work of art that richly meditates on relationships between opposites, between authenticity and performance, reality and dream, abyss and pattern. As part of this work, they constitute especially dense forms of being, sites that through their paradoxical natures gesture toward the paradoxical silence behind all utterance, the empty yet full gulf generating all discernible creatures. Hence, the dream featuring Betty and Rita—like the dreams of Guillaume, Chaucer, and the Pearl poet—is an illusion pointing to a truth, a wisp revealing sacred life.

Conspiracy Theory

The dream featuring Betty and Rita is indeed "Gnostic," a tale revealing the secret abyss from which all forms flow. Specifically, this narrative strain depicts how these two women find their sacred identities in the face of a tyrannical demiurge bent on killing Rita and ignoring Betty. This is the great struggle of the dream—between those who attempt to reduce experience to their egotistical wills and those who open to the transformative mysteries of existence. In trying to construct their own reality, the former group guarantees that they will live only in a dream divorced from the real. In endeavoring to open to energies beyond the ego, the latter group entertains the possibility of experiencing a dream that unveils reality.

As we have seen, the film early on shows two men bent on killing Rita. Soon after she escapes, Mr. Roque, the man with the small head and the thin mustache, inaugurates a series of phone calls that ostensibly end in a call to a man who might hunt down and possibly kill Rita. In his self-contained chamber and elevated chair, with his ability to give orders and expect them to be carried out immediately, Mr. Roque appears as nothing less than a little god, a godling, as it were, capable of directing the affairs of the entire Hollywood scene.[13] He not only directs the effort to find and potentially eliminate Rita, he also is behind a campaign to replace Rita on the film in which she was ostensibly cast. Early in the film, a meeting in a Hollywood boardroom is staged. In this meeting, two men, the Castigliane brothers (Dan Hedaya and Angelo Badalamenti), enter silently and rudely into the room. One of the men simply removes a picture from a briefcase and claims, indifferently, "This is the girl." The director of the film, Adam Kesher (Justin Theroux), is outraged. He chafes mightily at the idea that someone might control his ability to cast his own film. Unfazed, the brother repeats his claim, "This is the girl." Adam leaves the room in a huff. In the parking lot, he smashes the windshield of the Castigliane brothers' car, and drives away.

The meaning of these scenes appears to be this: Mr. Roque has apparently decided that the director Adam needs to cast another girl in his film, one Camilla Rhodes. To make sure that this happens, he arranges to have Rita, the initial cast member, killed. Though he fails to have Rita removed, he nonetheless in her absence—she has gone missing—arranges to cast another girl in the movie. Mr. Roque has the power to make this happen. Then, Adam smashes the window of the Castigliane brothers' car, he discovers that the entire production has been shut down and that all of his bank accounts have been frozen. Then, Adam finds out that he needs to meet a cowboy (Monty Montgomery) on an abandoned ranch above the city. During a bizarre interview during which this cowboy scolds Adam for his bad attitude, Adam learns that he can resume filming the very next day if he says, simply,

"This is the girl" after Camilla Rhodes (here played by Melissa George; later she will be played by Laura Elena Harring) has performed her audition. Adam agrees to do so. The next day he finds himself on a soundstage. After several auditions, Rhodes appears. Just as she finishes her number, Betty walks into the staging area with a casting agent. She has just completed her wonderfully erotic audition, and the casting agent wants her to meet Adam. The agent believes that Betty is perfect for the vacated role. Just before Adam officially casts Camilla, he notices Betty. Clearly enamored, he does a double take. Just before Betty can walk up to meet Adam, she leaves for an appointment with Rita. Two paths almost meet but never cross. Betty, it appears, has missed her big chance because of the machinations of Mr. Roque.[14]

Mr. Roque plays the Gnostic demiurge. He organizes the experiences of the fallen, fragmented world. He bends time and space to fit his fancies and thus oppresses others at every turn. His arm reaches as high as the Hollywood boardroom and as low as the two-bit hit man. He puts Adam the artistic genius under his vulgar control. He tries to kill Rita when she doesn't suit his ends. His machinations exclude Betty from the movie stardom that she deserves. His force is ubiquitous.

In playing the demiurge, Mr. Roque attempts to flatten experience to meet the whims of his narrow ego. He is an imperialist of experience, someone who reduces every event to his will to power. While this practice might lead to earthly power, it ultimately results in solipsism, to looking at phenomena and seeing only oneself. In this situation, the world turns mirror. One sees only distorted and reversed images of his own visage. He dwells solely in the limited illusions of his own making, the paltry images of his vulgar ego. He is a bad artist, attenuating the world to one ugly face. His visions are tawdry, mere fantasies of infantile control. His characters are flat, predictable.

Betty and Rita rebel against his mode of experiencing the world. Both resemble Gnostics, those who know that time and space are much richer and more complex than the power-hungry executives would have us believe. In contrast to Mr. Roque, Betty and Rita are open to otherness, to strange and new experiences that might change their egos once and for all. These two women are indeed connoisseurs of experience, lovers of the aesthetic fecundity of each other and of their environment. Their modes of perception result not in solipsism but in charity, in gazing outward with a generous spirit. Construed from this perspective, the world becomes a window as much as a mirror, a site where self and other, identity and difference, projection and perception, meet and merge. The illusions resulting from this interplay are always gatherings of oppositions, dynamic interplays between ego and unconscious, pattern and abyss. To base one's life on these images is to become a good artist, to embody in one's gestures the ordered chaos, the discordant concord, of the universe. Living this way, one makes life art, and reality a splendid dream—a durable and full-blooded reverie of hope.

Waking to a Dream

Mulholland Dr. does not conclude with the sweetly sad gnosis of Rita and Betty. As we have seen, Rita and Betty disappear when the blue key enters the blue box. This blue box is obviously some kind of transitional contraption, a vehicle moving one perhaps from dream to reality, perhaps from one kind of dream to another. On the surface, it appears that this box signals a waking. Just after Betty and Rita vanish, the cowboy who schooled Adam appears in the apartment of Diane Selwyn. He tells a woman sleeping on red sheets that it's time to wake up. Though she resembles the dead woman discovered by Betty and Rita, she awakens. She turns out to be the same woman as Betty—albeit in a less attractive, less charismatic form. Diane indeed lives in a dirty and sordid apartment, wears a ratty old robe, suffers from bad teeth, and has disheveled hair.[15]

It appears that this woman has been asleep for a long time and that the dream of Betty and Rita was her fantasy of wish fulfillment. Several details of the last third of the film suggest this interpretation. First, Betty is everything that Diane is not. Where Betty is ebullient and charismatic, Diane is dowdy and sour. Where Betty enjoys the erotic affection of Rita, Diane suffers rejection from the same woman as Rita, now named Camilla Rhodes (and played now, as mentioned earlier, by Laura Elena Harring).[16]

Where Betty is an excellent actress passed over through no fault of her own, Diane is a struggling performer who gets bit parts only through Camilla's influence. Where Diane helps Rita find her identity, the bitter Diane hires a hit man to kill Camilla. Moreover, several images and characters in the "dream" show up in Diane's "real" life. The mysterious blue key of the "dream" appears as a regular house key in "reality." The key is not a marker of the transition between sleeping and waking, though; rather, it's a sign that the hit Diane ordered has been completed. The same blue box appears, too. In the "dream" it's obviously, like the key, a vehicle of transition between dream and reality; in "reality," it shows up in the hands of a horrifically evil-looking homeless man and unleashes the forms that will eventually lead to Diane's terrible end. The same black handbag makes an appearance as well; this time, the bag is not the bearer of mysterious money but contains the cold hard cash that Diane pays the hit man. In the "dream," this hit man was hired to find and kill Rita; here, he is hired to track down and knock off Camilla. In the "dream," Betty is of course the spunky detective and lover of Rita; here, she is simply a waitress at a cafe. More characters appear in both realms: Adam, the cowboy, the girl named Camilla in the "dream," and the "dream's" apartment manager. Motifs recur as well. The phrase "This is the girl" appears at least four times in the "dream"; in "reality," it also appears when Diane, while talking to the hit man, points to a picture of Camilla and says, "This is the girl." Terrible evil shows up in the "dream" in the form of the devilish figure behind the diner; this same figure shows up in "reality" as well, and also appears to symbolize unspeakable evil there. Likewise, the limo driving over Mulholland Dr. is in both "dream" and "reality." In both, it carries a woman on the verge of descending into terrible danger in the city below. In the "dream," it releases the terrified and bewildered Rita into an L.A. cityscape where hit men hunt her down; in "reality," it releases an emotionally vulnerable Diane into an L.A. party where Camilla maliciously rubs her nose in the fact that she's marrying Adam. Finally, the old couple show up in "dream" and "reality"; in both realms, they seem to betoken the difficulty in telling the difference between appearance and reality. In the "dream," they laugh in a sinister fashion after kindly chatting with Betty in the airport. In "reality," they emerge as small creatures from the blue box held by the monstrous man living behind the diner; though they appear again to be the kindly old couple, they track down Diane, slip under her door, reach full size, and hound her back into her room. There, maddened, she kills herself.

All of these details ostensibly show that the "dream" is Diane's wish fulfillment, her effort both to imagine a better life for herself— one in which she gets the love of the woman called Camilla—and to account for her failure as an actress—a conspiracy keeps her from getting the roles she thinks she deserves. But the sequences in which Diane is depicted are far more "dreamy" than is the narrative featuring Betty and Rita; that is, they are more nonlinear, fragmented, and visionary. First of all, time is out of joint. Diane wakes up to find the blue key on her coffee table, the sign that Camilla has been killed. Then, the film immediately jumps to a jumbled series of events that seem to have taken place before this moment. We witness Diane watch Camilla make out with Adam on the movie set; we see Diane at the engagement party for Camilla; we watch Diane hire the hit man. We don't know which of these events comes first or second or third. These events are moreover overlapped with the ostensible present. Second, the film at this juncture unfolds in quick, episodic bits, in short, unpredictable takes. The effect is bewildering, vertiginous. Finally, Diane during these sequences persistently has visions that may or may not be real. She on two occasions believes that she's back with Camilla, that the two of them, scantily clad, are making love on the couch. In these moments, her sordid apartment and dowdy appearance are respectively transformed into a beautiful chamber and an attractive figure. One of these occasions appears to be generated by Diane's masturbatory fantasy, but we cannot tell for sure. At another time, as we have seen, the miniature old man and old woman slide under Diane's door, grow to full size, and press her back into her apartment. This crazy event makes her take out a gun and kill herself, seemingly out of an insane guilt over having her former lover killed.

This confusion over whether Diane's life is real or a dream is compounded by the film's ending. After Diane kills herself, becoming in that instant the dead woman in the narrative of Betty and Rita, the film returns to a shot of the illuminated Betty at the end of the jitterbug contest. It then shows Betty and Rita together, in an equally luminous light. Both have blonde hair. The movie then features the empty interior of the Club Silencio. In a box seat, only one person appears, a woman with white makeup and vivid blue hair. She says, simply, "Silencio." The film then ends.

The return of these images is confusing. If Diane is now dead, why would her dream images appear on the screen? The appearance of these images suggests that Diane might not have been the dreamer of Betty and Rita at all. If so, then who was? Another question occurs—if Diane's sequence is a dream and not reality, then who is her dreamer? Is one dreamer behind both the Betty sequence and the Diane sequence? Again, who would this dreamer be? Could it be someone unknown, a kind of ideal dreamer who could never actually exist? Or could it be David Lynch himself?

We can never of course know the answer to any of these questions, but we can conjecture this: *Mulholland Dr.* might well be one dreamer's dream of two modes of dreaming. This dreamer could well be David Lynch or some ideal dreamer. In any case, if *Mulholland Dr.* is all one dream, it features a contrast between the kind of dream that is open to the abysmal currents of silence and the kind of dream that is egocentrically closed to these same energies. The dream of Betty and Rita is, as we know, a long meditation on what composes an ideal self and on what relationship exists between original silence and copied sounds. In exploring these elements, it also depicts contrasting themes: what constitutes a narrow, egocentric self, and what connection exists between tyranny and perception. In the end, the dream is a Gnostic contemplation on how self-knowledge relates to the generative abyss, on how sacred identity emerges from an apprehension of the sacred origin of all phenomena. In contrast, the dream of Diane is a brief depiction of an egocentric self attempting to control experience through violence. In this way, the dream resembles the Mr. Roque conspiracy in the dream of Betty and Rita. Like Mr. Roque, Diane cannot open to a world beyond her ego. She must reduce experience to her sense of how the world should be, even if it means killing a lover. Ultimately, her dream is an anti-Gnostic nightmare, a detailing of the madness that occurs when one is divorced from the abyss of life and enclosed only in the narrow, scared ego.

All of these readings must remain highly tentative. Lynch puts viewers in the same position as he puts Rita and Betty. We must become detectives lost in the midst of life's deepest mysteries. We can never know, it seems, if we are awake or asleep, real or recorded. This doesn't mean, however, that existence is meaningless. On the contrary, some dreams, even if they are not empirically real, might show us the way to salvation—to a full and harmonious being, to a deep font of the cosmos. This is a dangerous and problematical claim. It suggests that fantasies are the only facts, that somnambulistic whims dictate even death. There is no firm footing in this field of dreams. We are actors in a film whose script has been lost and whose director is gone. But this skepticism, treacherous as it is, at least offers this one enduring solace, however slight. There is no such thing as matter in this plane of reverie, only the wisps and films of the sporadic mind. There is only impalpable figure; there is only ghostly form. Hence, something like freedom exists in this phantom ecology, something like spirit. Even though we are dreams, at least, perhaps, we can dream what we want. Even though we are not palpably real, at least, potentially, we dwell with playful spirit, the light of day's night.

NOTES

1. Chris Rodley, ed., *Lynch on Lynch*, rev. ed. (New York: Faber & Faber, 2005), 287.

2. Rodley claims that the film is a quest for identity (ibid., 267).

3. Rodley says that it's hard to tell what is dream and what's reality. The first two-thirds of the film, seemingly a dream, are "coherent and fluid" (ibid.). The last third of the film, apparently reality, is "discontinuous, abstracted, and fevered" (ibid.).

4. Contance B. Hieatt, *The Realism of Dream Visions: The Poetic Exploitation of the Dream-Experience in Chaucer and his Contemporaries* (Paris: Mouton & Co., 1967), 27–29; A. C. Spearing, *Medieval Dream Poetry* (New York: Cambridge University Press, 1976), 8–10.

5. Hieatt, *Realism of Dream Visions,* 29–30.

6. Jennifer A. Hudson nicely captures Lynch's ambiguity here. She says that Lynch, like poststructuralists, "sees reality as fluid, expansive, and in constant motion, and he resists inscribing reality within a system of linguistic signs he views as hollow and unstable" ("'No Hay Banda, and Yet We Hear A Band': David Lynch's Reversal of Coherence in *Mulholland Drive,*" *Journal of Film and Video* 56, no. 11 [Spring 2004]: 19).

7. Friedrich Nietzsche, *The Birth of Tragedy Out of the Spirit of Music,* in *Basic Writings of Nietzsche,* trans. Walter Kaufmann, 3–146 (New York: Modern Library, 1968), 33–38.

8. Ibid., 33, 47.

9. C. G. Jung makes this point in many places, but very concisely, as Anthony Storr points out ("Introduction," in *The Essential Jung,* 13–28 [Princeton: Princeton University Press, 1983], 19), in *Alchemical Studies,* trans. R. F. C. Hull, in *Collected Works of C. G. Jung,* vol. 13 (Princeton: Princeton University Press, 1967), 45–46.

10. Hudson succinctly addresses the difficulty of ascertaining who is who in the film—who is the dreamer and who is the dream? Is the dreamer one or two? She writes, in the movie, realities "are juxtaposed, identities shift and merge, and unsettled viewers find themselves taking on the role of detective" ("'No Hay Banda,'" 17).

11. What Hudson says of Rita also pertains to Betty. She and Betty alike epitomize "the vagueness of conceptual borders, confusion of place, and incoherence that have become staples of Lynch's aesthetics" (ibid., 20). Neither character has a "fixed self" (ibid.).

12. I think that this idea is to some extent what Martha P. Nochimson has in mind when she claims that Lynch believes that "the culture industry has options for producing authentic public dreams" ("Review of *Mulholland Drive,*" *Film Quarterly* 56, no. 1 [Autumn 2002]: 39).

13. Nochimson calls Roque "a lord of a static void cut off from the ebb and flow of creative energy" (ibid.).

14. Nochimson claims that this moment shows that *Mulholland Dr.,* like *Lost Highway,* shows a new trend in Lynch's cinema—the depiction of "protagonists who miss their moment" (ibid.). To a great extent, I agree with this claim, though I show how in both films Lynch still holds a ray of hope, the possibility that these characters might have, in a certain sense, not missed their moment at all.

15. Todd McGowan applies the same Lacanian logic to *Mulholland Dr.* that he applied to *Lost Highway.* He argues that the first part of the film is a depiction of fantasy—or desire fulfilled—and the second part is a portrait of desire—desire thwarted ("Lost on *Mulholland Drive*: Navigating David Lynch's Panegyric to Hollywood," *Cinema Journal* 43, no. 2 [2004]: 67–89).

16. Kelly McDowell argues that the dream in the first two-thirds of the film is a revelation of Diane's unconscious—specifically, her "unresolved

oedipal conflicts that have led to her sadomasochistic relationship with Camilla, who functions as the mother-figure in the oedipus conflict" ("Unleashing the Feminine Unconscious: Female Oedipal Desires and Lesbian Sadomasochism in *Mulholland Dr.*," *The Journal of Popular Culture* 38, no. 6 [2005]: 1038). This is an interesting reading, but it doesn't account for the fact that the last third of the film might well be a dream as well.

CONCLUSION

David Lynch's Nihilism

L ynch's work increasingly moves toward this conclusion: there are no absolute truths, only quick experiences. This conclusion would appear to suggest nothing but nihilism, the idea that no enduring values pervade the universe. Generally, nihilism is anathema, an extremely dangerous vision that leads in most cases to philosophical and even physical anarchy, a sense that anything goes, that nothing is worth living for. But such interpretations of nihilism might well be shortsighted. Is there another way of viewing this worldview—this idea that no permanent truths, no persistent essences, exist? Is there a path to seeing this form of perception as a necessary corrective to fundamentalist positions, to religious imperialisms, to fanaticisms of all stamps?

Against bitter nihilism—the sort that says, angrily, that life is merely meaningless—let us set generous nihilism. This kind of nihilism is something like a gentle skepticism, an openhearted sense that nothing is certain, that nothing is inevitable, that nothing is, finally, once and for all, real. Such skepticism is not hopeless, but purgative. It purifies the mind and the heart from metaphysical and psychological clutter, from those alleged sureties that shut down seeking, that result in complacency, in rigidity. Such clutter is not idle; it is a type of death, a trading of contingent development for stiff linearity, of creative difference for mere repetition, of organ for machine. To remove this mental and emotional mess is to open to the strange particulars of existence, to the weird nuances, the new complexities. Such elements can make life dynamic, tense, curious.

But can we not go down to a little lower layer? In opening to the vital impermanence of life, does not this kind of tender-hearted nihilism witness something else again? Doesn't this form of nihilism stand, literally, before nothing, no-*thing*? Things are of course abstractions, constructed frames around the flows and smokes of time. To see the world suddenly as a field of flux, a current of energy, is to apprehend a realm devoid of things, to perceive the universe as no-thing. What is this no-*thing*, but, possibly, *no*-thing? What is no-thing, but, perhaps, the Nothing, the void from which all form arises, the plenitude out of which passing comes, the silence preceding and informing all sound? Nihilism in this sense is a Gnosticism, a religion, a vision of the world not as an arrangement of static stuff but as a secret spiritual river, a baptism of unseen waters.

These are bold and probably untenable thoughts, but they are nonetheless the very ideas toward which Lynch's ironic religion points us. Lynch averts our gaze from fundamentalism—from Frank's rage for order, from the tyranny of Fred—turns our eyes toward openhearted questing—toward the investigating of Jeffrey, the transcendence of Pete. Lynch in his films indeed fosters a sort of charitable skepticism. This skepticism keeps thought and feeling fresh and alive, agitated by doubt and buoyed by faith. If this skepticism opens us to the contingencies and pulses of the living, then, we can say, all the better. If it takes us into the abyss originating and informing creatures, then, well, even better. Though we can never know for sure what this skepticism produces, we can at least find some comfort, however tense, in this: we have chosen seeking over stasis.

As I write this, Lynch is completing his filming of his latest movie, *Inland Empire*. At this point, no one knows much about the picture. Characteristically, Lynch is tight-lipped about his script, saying only that the film is the story of "a woman in deep trouble" and that the story is also "a hidden mystery." Whatever the content, we can be fairly certain that the film, like all of Lynch's other religious movies, will explore the mystery of the inland, of the imperial interiors that stay forever unmapped. In undertaking yet again the task of sounding the abysmal insides of the heart, this picture will no doubt deepen Lynch's nihilistic vision—his religion of no religion, his ironic transcendence.

Filmography

Blue Velvet. Dir. David Lynch. Perfs. Kyle McLachlan, Dennis Hopper, Isabella Rossellini, Laura Dern. De Laurentiis Entertainment Group, 1986.

Dune. Dir. David Lynch. Perfs. Kyle MacLachlan, Francesca Annis, Jürgen Prochnow. De Laurentiis, Universal Films, 1984.

The Elephant Man. Dir. David Lynch. Perfs. John Hurt, Anthony Hopkins, Anne Bancroft. Brooksfilms, Ltd., 1980.

Eraserhead. Dir. David Lynch. Perfs. Jack Nance, Charlotte Stewart, Allen Joseph. American Film Institute, Libra Films, 1977.

Lost Highway. Dir. David Lynch. Perfs. Bill Pullman, Patricia Arquette, Balthazar Getty. Asymmetrical Productions, CiBy 2000, Lost Highway Productions, LLC, October Films, 1997.

Mulholland Dr. Dir. David Lynch. Perfs. Naomi Watts, Laura Harring, Justin Theroux. Les Film Alain Sarde, Asymmetrical Productions, Babbo Inc., Canal +, The Picture Factory, 2001.

Six Men Getting Sick. Dir. David Lynch. *The Short Films of David Lynch.* www.davidlynch.com, 2002.

The Straight Story. Dir. David Lynch. Perfs. Richard Farnsworth, Sissy Spacek, Harry Dean Stanton. Asymmetrical Productions, Canal +, Channel Four Films, CiBy 2000, Les Films Alain Sarde, The Picture Factory, The Straight Story, Inc., Walt Disney Pictures, 1999.

Twin Peaks: Fire Walk with Me. Dir. David Lynch. Perfs. Sheryl Lee, Ray Wise, Kyle MacLachlan. New Line Cinema, CiBy 2000, 1992.

Wild at Heart. Dir. David Lynch. Perfs. Nicholas Cage, Laura Dern, Diane Ladd. PolyGram Film Entertainment, Propaganda Films, 1990.

Bibliography

Alexander, John. *The Films of David Lynch*. London: Charles Letts, 1993.

Atkinson, Michael. *Blue Velvet*. London: British Film Institute, 1997.

Berry, Betsy. "Forever, In My Dreams: Generic Conventions and the Subversive Imagination in *Blue Velvet*." *Literature/Film Quarterly* 16, no. 2 (1988): 82–90.

Biga, Tracy. "Review of *Blue Velvet*." *Film Quarterly* 41, no. 1 (Autumn 1987): 44–49.

Bird, Michael. "Film as Hierophany." In *Religion in Film*, edited by John R. May and Michael Bird, 3–22. Knoxville: University of Tennessee Press, 1982.

Briffault, Robert S. *The Troubadours*. Bloomington: Indiana University Press, 1965.

Campbell, Joseph. *The Masks of God: Creative Mythology*. New York: Penguin, 1968.

Carabine, Deirdre. *The Unknown God: Negative Theology in the Platonic Tradition, Plato to Eriugena*. Louvain, Belgium: Peeters Press, 1995.

Chion, Michel. *David Lynch*. London: British Film Institute, 1995.

Coughlin, Paul. "*Blue Velvet*: Postmodern Parody and the Subversion of Conservative Frameworks." *Literature/Film Quarterly* 31, no. 4 (2003): 304–11.

Creed, Barbara. "A Journey through *Blue Velvet*: Film, Fantasy, and the Female Spectator." *New Formations* 7 (1988): 95–115.

Culiano, Ioan P. *The Tree of Gnosis: Gnostic Mythology from Early Christianity to Modern Nihilism*. New York: HarperCollins, 1992.

Denzin, Norman K. *Images of Postmodern Society: Social Theory and Contemporary Cinema*. London: Sage, 1991.

Duerr, Hans Peter. *Dreamtime: Concerning the Boundary between Wilderness and Civilization*. Oxford: Blackwell, 1987.

169

Dunne, Michael. "*Wild at Heart* in Three Ways: Lynch, Gifford, Bahktin." *Literature/Film Quarterly* 23, no. 1 (1995): 6–13.

Falsani, Cathleen. "Lynch: 'Bliss Is Our Nature.'" *Chicago Sun Times*, January 16, 2005, http://www.lynchnet.com/articles/suntimes.html.

Frye, Northrop. *A Natural Perspective: The Development of Shakespearean Comedy and Romance.* New York: Harcourt, Brace, Jovanovich, 1965.

Gillet, Louis. *Dante.* Paris: Flammarion, 1941.

Godwin, K. George. "Review of *Eraserhead.*" *Film Quarterly* 39, no. 1 (Autumn 1985): 37–43.

Gore, Chris. "David Lynch Interview: Is David Just a Little Weird?" *Film Threat*, January 17, 2000, http://www.filmthreat.com/Interviews .asp?Id=3.

Hainge, Fred. "Weird or Loopy? Specular Spaces, Feedback, and Artifice in *Lost Highway*'s Aesthetics of Sensation." In *The Cinema of David Lynch: American Dreams, Nightmare Visions*, edited by Erica Sheen and Annette Davison, 136–50. New York: Wallflower Press, 2005.

Hampton, Howard. "David Lynch's Secret History of the United States." *Film Comment* 29, no. 3 (1993): 37–41, 47.

Haule, John. *Divine Madness.* Boston: Shambhala, 1990.

Heidegger, Martin. *On Time and Being.* Translated by Joan Stambaugh. New York: Harper & Row, 1972.

Herzogenrath, Bernd. "On the *Lost Highway*: Lynch and Lacan, Cinema and Cultural Pathology." *Other Voices* 1, no. 3 (January 1999), http://www.othervoices.org/1.3/bh/highway.html.

Hieatt, Constance B. *The Realism of Dream Visions: The Poetic Exploitation of the Dream-Experience in Chaucer and His Contemporaries.* Paris: Mouton & Co., 1967.

Hudson, Jennifer A. "'No Hay Banda, and Yet We Hear A Band': David Lynch's Reversal of Coherence in *Mulholland Drive.*" *Journal of Film and Video* 56, no. 11 (Spring 2004): 17–24.

Ishii-Gonzales, Sam. "Mysteries of Love: Lynch's *Blue Velvet*/Freud's Wolf-Man." In *The Cinema of David Lynch: American Dreams, Nightmare Visions*, edited by Erica Sheen and Annette Davison, 48–60. New York: Wallflower Press, 2005.

Jerslev, Anne. "Beyond Boundaries: David Lynch's *Lost Highway.*" In *The Cinema of David Lynch: American Dreams, Nightmare Visions*, edited by Erica Sheen and Annette Davison, 151–64. New York: Wallflower Press, 2005.

Johnson, Jeff. *Pervert in the Pulpit: Morality in the Works of David Lynch.* West Jefferson, NC: MacFarland, 2004.

Jonas, Hans. *The Gnostic Religion*. 3rd ed. Boston: Beacon, 2001.

Jung, C. G. *Alchemical Studies*, translated by R. F. C. Hull. In *Collected Works of C. G. Jung*, vol. 13. Princeton: Princeton University Press, 1967.

Kaleta, Kenneth. *David Lynch*. New York: Twayne, 1993.

Kant, Immanuel. *Critique of Judgment*. Translated by Werner S. Pluhar. Indianapolis: Hackett, 1987.

Lacarriere, Jacques. *The Gnostics*. San Francisco: City Lights Press, 1989.

Layton, Bentley, trans. *The Gnostic Scriptures: Ancient Wisdom for the New Age*. New York: Doubleday, 1987.

Layton, Lynne. "*Blue Velvet*: A Parable of Male Development." *Screen* 35, no. 4 (1994): 374–93.

Lindroth, James. "Down the Yellow Brick Road: Two Dorothys and the Journey of Initiation in Dream and Nightmare." *Literature/Film Quarterly* 18, no. 3 (1990): 160–66.

McDowell, Kelly. "Unleashing the Feminine Unconscious: Female Oedipal Desires and Lesbian Sadomasochism in *Mulholland Dr.*" *The Journal of Popular Culture* 38, no. 6 (2005): 1037–49.

McGowan, Todd. "Finding Ourselves on a 'Lost Highway': David Lynch's Lesson in Fantasy." *Cinema Journal* 39, no. 2 (2000): 51–73.

———. "Lost on *Mulholland Drive*: Navigating David Lynch's Panegyric to Hollywood." *Cinema Journal* 43, no. 2 (2004): 67–89.

McKinney, Devin. "Review of *Wild at Heart*." *Film Quarterly* 45, no. 2 (Winter 1991–92): 41–46.

Moon, Michael. "A Small Boy and Others: Sexual Disorientation in Henry James, Kenneth Ager, and David Lynch." In *Comparative American Identities: Race, Sex, and Nationality in the Modern Text*, edited by Hortense J. Spillers, 141–56. New York: Routledge, 1991.

Mulvey, Laura. "The Pre-Oedipal Father: The Gothicism and *Blue Velvet*." In *Modern Gothic: A Reader*, edited by Victor Sage and Allan Lloyd Smith, 38–57. New York: Manchester University Press, 1996.

Murphy, Kathleen. "Dead Heat on a Merry-Go-Round." *Film Comment* 26, no. 6 (November 1990): 59–62.

Nelson, Victoria. *The Secret Life of Puppets*. Cambridge, MA: Harvard University Press, 2002.

Nietzsche, Friedrich. *The Birth of Tragedy Out of the Spirit of Music*. In *Basic Writings of Nietzsche*, translated by Walter Kaufmann, 3–146. New York: Modern Library, 1968.

Nochimson, Martha P. "'All I Need Is the Girl': The Life and Death of Creativity in *Mulholland Drive*." In *The Cinema of David Lynch:*

American Dreams, Nightmare Visions, edited by Erica Sheen and Annette Davis, 165–181. New York: Wallflower Press, 2005.

———. *The Passion of David Lynch: Wild at Heart in Hollywood*. Austin: University of Texas Press, 1997.

———. "Review of *Mulholland Drive*." *Film Quarterly* 56, no. 1 (Autumn 2002): 37–45.

O'Connor, Tom. "The Pitfalls of Media 'Representations': David Lynch's *Lost Highway*." *The Journal of Film and Video* 57, no. 3 (Fall 2005): 14–30.

Otto, Rudolph. *The Idea of the Holy: An Inquiry into the Non-Rational Factor in the Idea of the Divine and Its Relation to the Rational*. Translated by John W. Harvey. Oxford: Oxford University Press, 1923.

Pagels, Elaine. *The Gnostic Gospels*. New York: Vintage, 1989.

Pfeil, Fred. "Home Fires Burning: Family *Noir* in *Blue Velvet* and *Terminator 2*." In *Shades of Noir*, edited by Joan Copjec, 227–60. New York: Verso, 1993.

Preston, Janet. "Dantean Imagery in *Blue Velvet*." *Literature/ Film Quarterly* 18, no. 3 (1990): 167–72.

Rhodes, Eric Bryant. "Review of *Lost Highway*." *Film Quarterly* 51, no. 3 (Spring 1998): 57–61.

Rodley, Chris, ed. *Lynch on Lynch*. Rev. ed. New York: Faber & Faber, 2005.

Rombes, Nicholas. "*Blue Velvet* Underground: David Lynch's Post-Punk Poetics." In *The Cinema of David Lynch: American Dreams, Nightmare Visions*, edited by Erica Sheen and Annette Davis, 61–76. New York: Wallflower Press, 2005.

Rudolph, Kurt. *Gnosis: The Nature and History of Gnosticism*. Rev. ed. San Francisco: HarperSanFrancisco, 1987.

Rushdie, Salmon. *The Wizard of Oz*. London: British Film Institute, 1992.

Schiller, Friedrich. *Letters on the Aesthetic Education of Man*. Translated by Reginald Snell. New York: Frederick Ungar, 1965.

Schlegel, Friedrich. *Philosophical Fragments*. Translated by Peter Firchow. Minneapolis: University of Minnesota Press, 1991.

Schneider, Steven Jay. "The Essential Evil in/of *Eraserhead* (or, Lynch to the Contrary)." In *The Cinema of David Lynch: American Dreams, Nightmare Visions*, edited by. Erica Sheen and Annette Davis, 5–18. New York: Wallflower Press, 2005.

Schrader, Paul. *Transcendental Style in Film: Ozu, Bresson, Dreyer*. New York: Da Capo, 1972.

Spearing, A. C. *Medieval Dream Poetry*. New York: Cambridge University Press, 1976.

Storr, Anthony. "Introduction." In *The Essential Jung*, edited by Anthony Storr, 13–28. Princeton: Princeton University Press, 1983.

Vasilev, Georgi. "Bogomills, Cathars, Lollards, and the High Social Position of Women During the Middles Ages." *Facta Universitatis* 2, no. 7 (2000): 325–36, http://facta.junis.ni.ac.yu/facta/pas/pas2000/pas2000-02.pdf.

Warner, Marina. "Voodoo Road: David Lynch's New Identity-swap Chiller *Lost Highway* Reflects the Fractured Image of the Modern Narcissus." *Sight and Sound* 7, no. 8 (1997): 6–11.

Williams, Michael Allen. *Rethinking "Gnosticism": An Argument for Dismantling a Dubious Category*. Princeton: Princeton University Press, 1996.

Wilson, Eric G. *Secret Cinema: Gnostic Vision in Film*. New York: Continuum, 2006.

Wittenberg, Judith Bryant, and Robert Gooding-Williams. "The 'Strange World' of *Blue Velvet*: Conventions, Subversions, and Representations of Women." In *Sexual Politics and Popular Culture*, edited by Diane Raymond, 149–57. Bowling Green, KY: Bowling Green State University Popular Press, 1990.

Woods, Paul A. *Weirdsville, USA: The Obsessive Universe of David Lynch*. London: Plexus, 2000.

Woodward, Richard B. "Dark Lens on America." *New York Times Magazine*, January 15, 1990, 18–22.

Žižek, Slajov. *The Art of the Ridiculous Sublime: On David Lynch's* Lost Highway. Seattle: University of Washington Press, 2000.

Index